WITHDRAWN

The
Belgian
Sheepdog

Compiled and Edited by
William W. Denlinger and R. Annabel Rathman

Cover Design by
Bob Groves

by
Marge Turnquist

DENLINGER'S PUBLISHERS, LTD.
Box 76, Fairfax, Virginia 22030

Library of Congress Cataloging in Publication Data

Turnquist, Marge.
   The Belgian Sheepdog.

   1. Belgian sheepdog. I. Denlinger, William
Watson,   II. Rathman, R. Annabel.
III. Title.
SF429.B4T87   1985   686.7'3   88-25281
ISBN 0-87714-102-9

International Standard Book Number: 0-87714-102-9

Established 1926

DENLINGER'S *Publishers, Ltd.*

Publisher
Wm. W. Denlinger
Editor-In-Chief
R. Annabel Rathman

703-631-1500
P. O. Box 76
Fairfax, Va.
22030

THE BELGIAN SHEEPDOG   By Marge Turnquist

C O R R E C T I O N S

Please take note of the following corrections to this publication:

Page 18, captions were inadvertently switched for the drawings showing incorrect and correct angulation. The drawing showing 90° angulation should be captioned as correct angulation and 120° angulation should be captioned as incorrect.

Page 38, captions were switched for the two lower photos. The dog pictured at left is Deagan Van Mell's Dark of Night and the dog on the right is Ch. Liza del Pirata Nero, C.D.

Acknowledgements

I would like to thank the former and present members of the Belgian Sheepdog Club of America for their support and for the pictures they provided for this book. A special thanks to our Club Historian, David Spang, for information from his records, and to Margery Riddle, for the use of old dog magazines.

This book is dedicated to Belgian Sheepdogs of the past, present, and future, with the hope that it will be an aid to first-time owners, and that the data and pictures will be of interest to experienced breeders.

"Belgians on the Skyline." From left to right: Thor, C.D.X., Bonita del Rio Carmello, and Ch. Hadji de Flanders, U.D.T., all owned by Mr. and Mrs. Bill Vestal. This was the one picture chosen by the Belgian Sheepdog Club of America to represent the breed in the Club's booklet.

Ch. Jaye's Von Jet. (A-Yacht's Happy Fella x A-Yacht's Quellette.) Owner, Elaine Jaye.

Contents

Reproduced on the front cover of this book is a photograph of Ch. Charro of Geier Tal.

On the back cover is "A Basketful of Trouble." Cheyenne Turk, seven weeks old, owned by Frank and Artice Mainville.

Chieho Belgian puppies. Owner, Elaine Jaye.

Selecting and Training a Belgian Sheepdog Puppy

The selection of a puppy of any breed to become a member of your household should be approached with caution and much consideration. All puppies are adorable when they are small—especially Belgians, which look like little black teddy bears—but they grow up fast. Belgians need plenty of exercise to develop properly and to run off excess energy. You should consider: Do you have ample space for the dog to exercise? Do you have time to give it the attention and discipline in the formative years that will make it a well-mannered, affectionate, devoted companion, or will it become a wild, undisciplined dog that is impossible to control or enjoy?

Take your time and find a breeder who has a reputation for being reliable and for dealing honestly with a prospective client. You can find the name and address of the secretary of the Belgian Sheepdog Club of America in the *American Kennel Gazette,* or you can write The American Kennel Club, at 51 Madison Avenue, New York, New York, 10010, for the information. The secretary may be able to direct you to breeders within driving distance of your home.

Make an appointment to see the puppies and the dam, and the sire if possible. Their actions can give you an idea of what you can expect when a puppy becomes an adult. If the sire or dam acts shy, backing away with its tail tucked between its legs and barking continually, you should visit another kennel.

If you do find a puppy, it will be much easier to bring him home with you and not risk the trauma of shipment by air. Take a dog crate with you to confine the puppy on the way home. A wire crate allows plenty of air circulation and the puppy will travel better if he can see people. This will make him feel that he is not alone and will give him confidence to deal with the new experience of riding in a car. Take plenty of newspaper to line the crate.

Before looking at the puppies, ask the breeder to bring out only the specimens of the sex you are interested in that are for sale. Trying to view an entire litter of puppies at once can be confusing. Some puppies will be cautious with strangers until they sense that all is well. It is best to get down on their level, sitting or squatting, because a strange person standing up can look pretty formidable. Never force yourself on a puppy, but let it come to you. Watch the puppies move about freely. Usually there is one that will catch your eye. Sometimes a puppy will choose you, and that will be a good choice, if it has the qualities that you are looking for.

The health of the puppy is the first consideration. The puppy should look well-cared for, full of life, playful, and friendly. The coat should be clean and free of parasites, and the eyes should be clear and alert, with no signs of discharge.

If you are picking a dog for a companion only, the choice is simpler. All you have to be concerned about is health and temperament. If you want a show prospect, the choice is more involved. You may want an older dog. Even an expert cannot accurately predict what a small puppy will look like when it matures. Characteristics which suggest show quality are substantial bone, good temperament, outgoing personality, sound body, compact feet, good coat, good teeth, and correct bite. Most breeders will be glad to point out the differences among puppies and will advise you of the puppies with show quality potential. Your best chance of getting a possible show quality puppy is to buy from a breeder whose lines have produced champions, and who also has been successful in show competition.

Papers

When you buy a purebred dog from anyone, regardless of that person's reputation, have all the terms of the agreement in writing before you leave with a puppy. Many breeders agree to let the puppy be checked by the

Warrah, seven weeks old. Owners, Frank and Artice Mainville. Photo by Frank Mainville.

7

purchaser's own veterinarian. If there is a problem, the purchaser can return the dog and the breeder will provide a replacement from the same litter, if available, or return the purchaser's money. Whatever agreement you work out must be in writing; otherwise, if the breeder does not live up to his part of the agreement, you do not have written proof should you take civil action or make a protest to The American Kennel Club for unethical conduct on the part of the breeder.

The breeder should provide you with the puppy's inoculation and worming records, a schedule for feeding, and information as to the type of food provided for the puppy. An abrupt change in food can cause diarrhea. The breeder should provide a pedigree of at least three generations and an American Kennel Club Registration Certificate, or an application form to fill out. Some breeders name and register each puppy individually. If this has been done, you will have to complete the transfer and send the form, with fee, to The American Kennel Club. The AKC will transfer the dog to your ownership and send you a new certificate. If you receive an application for registration from the breeder, you should fill it out, choosing a name for your dog, and mail it to The American Kennel Club with the correct fee, which will be listed on the application.

Coaltree's Kerry Ann. Owner, Pat Crabtree.

High-Mount's Kip of Hollandia at fourteen weeks. Owner, Helena Brown.

The Puppy's First Night in His New Home

The first night in your home can be a traumatic experience for both you and the puppy. This will be the puppy's first night away from his littermates, with whom he once cuddled up to sleep. He may be confused and frightened. The crate in which he was brought home can be a refuge. Cover the back half of the crate to create a dark place for him to rest.Line the crate with layers of paper. A loud-ticking alarm clock, placed by the crate, can be a comforting sound, and a radio with soft music will make the puppy feel that he is not completely alone. Give him a large milkbone to chew on in case he gets hungry. After a few nights he will adjust to his new home.

Health Check

Take your puppy to your veterinarian as soon as possible. Take a stool specimen for a worm check, and the worming and inoculation records provided by the breeder so that the veterinarian can continue the schedule for the inoculation series. Be sure to ask your veterinarian about heartworm medication, rabies shots, and other preventive inoculations the puppy will need. Take your veterinarian's advice and keep on schedule with his suggested program. If the veterinarian detects a serious problem in the puppy, notify the breeder immediately.

Ganymede Belgians, owned by Sheila and Lloyd Rentschler.

Dogs and Children

Dogs and children are a natural combination: they think alike, they act alike, and they train alike. Both have an abundance of energy that must be channeled in the right direction. Children should be taught to respect the rights of a puppy, just as they respect the rights of their playmates. They should not be allowed to maul a puppy or play until the puppy is exhausted. The best-natured puppy can finally lose his temper, if agitated persistently. A puppy needs rest periods in a place to which he can escape and rest undisturbed. Never let a child pounce on a sleeping dog. The dog may be startled, and since his first instinct is to protect himself, the child could receive a bad bite. Children should not be allowed to play tug of war with a young puppy by pulling against something the dog is holding in his mouth. This can pull the dog's mouth out of shape and cause damage to the teeth. It can also teach the dog the power of his teeth and lead to serious biting or to pulling on anything that offers resistance. A puppy should never be lifted up by his legs. The bones and ligaments have not matured and severe damage can occur.

If children and dogs are taught to play nicely together, it can be the most enjoyable time of their lives.

A puppy should never be allowed freedom of the house without constant supervision. Everything goes into a puppy's mouth. Certain house plants are poisonous. Cleaners and poisonous chemicals (under the sink, in most kitchens) can be lethal. Electrical outlet cords should always be disconnected or out of reach. Puppy teeth are sharp and can penetrate a cord easily, causing severe shock or death. If you are in the room and the puppy starts to chew on something he shouldn't, pick up a magazine or fly swatter, and while the puppy is not looking, either throw the magazine near him or bang the fly swatter on something to make a sharp noise as you give the command "NO!" If this is done so that it startles the dog, he will associate something unpleasant with chewing on objects of value or things that may result in harm to him. If the damage has been done while you are not present, do not punish him, because his memory is short and he has probably forgotten about it. It is all right to take him to the spot and ask in a firm tone of voice, "Did you do that? Bad dog!" Punishment depends on the dog's temperament. Some dogs learn from one bad experience, while others are more willful and have to be corrected repeatedly before they are convinced.

Voudoun's Pagan Jona An, C.D. and litter one hour after whelping. Owner, Kaye Hall.

Ch. Desiree de la Pouroffe winning the 1983 BSCA National Specialty in Las Vegas, Nevada, April 9, 1983. Judge, Judy Doniere. Handler, Ann Stornialo. Trophy presenter and show chairman, Chris Hyde. Breeder, Rene Renard, Noost, Belgium. Owners, Major and Mrs. Daniel E. Adams. Photo by Missy Yuhl.

Official Standard for the Belgian Sheepdog

Personality—The Belgian Sheepdog should reflect the qualities of intelligence, courage, alertness, and devotion to master. To his inherent aptitude as guardian of flocks should be added protectiveness of the person and property of his master. He should be watchful, attentive, and always in motion when not under command. In his relationship with humans he should be observant and vigilant with strangers but not apprehensive. He should not show fear or shyness. He should not show viciousness by unwarranted or unprovoked attack. With those he knows well, he is most affectionate and friendly, zealous of their attention, and very possessive.

General Appearance—The first impression of the Belgian Sheepdog is that of a well-balanced, square dog, elegant in appearance, with an exceedingly proud carriage of the head and neck. He is a strong, agile, well-muscled animal, alert and full of life. His whole conformation gives the impression of depth and solidity without bulkiness. The male dog is usually somewhat more impressive and grand than his female counterpart. The bitch should have a distinctly feminine look.

Size and Substance—Males should be 24-26 inches in height and females 22-24 inches, measured at the withers. The length, measured from point of breastbone to point of rump, should equal the height. Bitches may be slightly longer. Bone structure should be moderately heavy in proportion to his height so that he is well balanced throughout and neither spindly or leggy nor cumbersome and bulky. *Stance*—The Belgian Sheepdog should stand squarely on all fours. Side view: the topline, front legs, and back legs should closely approximate a square.

Expression—Indicates alertness, attention, readiness for activity. Gaze should be intelligent and questioning.

Coat—The guard hairs of the coat must be long, well-fitting, straight, and abundant. They should not be silky or wiry. The texture should be a medium harshness. The undercoat should be extremely dense, commensurate, however, with climatic conditions. The Belgian Sheepdog is particularly adaptable to extremes of temperature or climate. The hair is shorter on the head, outside of the ears, and lower part of the legs. The opening of the ear is protected by tufts of hair. *Ornamentation*—Especially long and abundant hair, like a collarette, around the neck; fringe of long hair down the back of the forearm; especially long and abundant hair trimming the hindquarters, the breeches; long, heavy, and abundant hair on the tail.

Color—Black. May be completely black or may be black with white, limited as follows: Small to moderate patch or strip on forechest. Between pads of feet. On *tips* of hind toes. On chin and muzzle (frost—may be white or gray). On *tips* of front toes—allowable but a fault.

Head—Clean-cut and strong, over-all size should be in proportion to the body. *Skull*—Top flattened rather than rounded. The width approximately the same, but not wider, than the length. *Stop*—Moderate. *Muzzle, Jaws, Lips*—Muzzle moderately pointed, avoiding any tendency to snipiness, and approximately equal in length to that of the topskull. The jaws should be strong and powerful. The lips should be tight and black, with no pink showing on the outside. *Ears*—Triangular in shape, stiff, erect, and in proportion to the head in size. Base of the ear should not come below the center of the eye. *Eyes*—Brown, preferably dark brown. Medium size, slightly almond shaped, not protruding. *Nose*—Black, without spots or discolored areas. *Teeth*—A full complement of strong, white teeth, evenly set. Should not be overshot or undershot. Should have either an even bite or a scissors bite.

Torso—*Neck*—Round and rather outstretched, tapered from head to body, well muscled, with tight skin. *Topline*—The withers are slightly higher and slope into the back which must be level, straight, and firm from withers to hip joints. The loin section, viewed from above, is relatively short, broad and strong, but blending smoothly into the back. The croup is medium long, sloping gradually. *Tail*—Strong at the base, bone to reach hock. At rest the dog holds it low, the tip bent back level with the hock. When in action he raises it and gives it a curl, which is strongest toward the tip, without forming a hook. *Chest*—Not broad, but deep. The lowest point should reach the elbow, forming a smooth ascendant curve to the abdomen. *Abdomen*—Moderate development. Neither tuck-up nor paunchy.

Forequarters—*Shoulder*—Long and oblique, laid flat against the body, forming a sharp angle (approximately 90°) with the upper arm. *Legs*—Straight, strong, and parallel to each other. Bone oval rather than round. Development (length and substance) should be well proportioned to the size of the dog. Pastern: Medium length, strong, and very slightly sloped. *Feet*—Round (cat-footed), toes curved close together, well padded. Nails strong and black except that they may be white to match white toe tips.

Hindquarters—*Thighs*—Broad and heavily muscled. The upper and lower thigh bones approximately parallel the shoulder blade and upper arm respectively, forming a relatively sharp angle at stifle joint. *Legs*—Length and substance well proportioned to the size of the dog. Bone oval rather than round. Legs are parallel to each other. The angle at the hock is relatively sharp, although the Belgian Sheepdog does not have extreme angulation. Metatarsus medium length, strong, and slightly sloped. Dewclaws, if any, should be removed. *Feet*—Slightly elongated. Toes curved close together, well padded. Nails strong and black except that they may be white to match white toe tips.

Gait—Motion should be smooth, free and easy, seemingly never tiring, exhibiting facility of movement rather than a hard driving action. He tends to single-track on a fast gait; the legs, both front and rear, converging toward the center line of gravity of the dog. The backline should remain firm and level, parallel to the line of motion with no crabbing. He shows a marked tendency to move in a circle rather than a straight line.

FAULTS

Any deviation from these specifications is a fault. In determining whether a fault is minor, serious, or major, these two factors should be used as a guide: 1. The extent to which it deviates from the Standard. 2. The extent to which such deviation would actually affect the working ability of the dog.

DISQUALIFICATIONS

Viciousness.

Ears—hanging (as on a hound).

Tail—cropped or stump.

Males under 22½ or over 27½ inches in height.

Females under 20½ or over 25½ inches in height.

Approved June 8, 1982

11

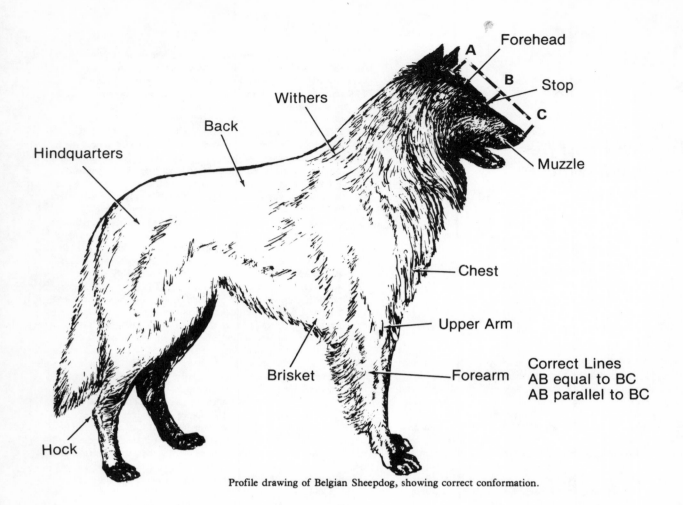

Hindquarters

Back

Withers

A **Forehead**

B **Stop**

C

Muzzle

Chest

Upper Arm

Brisket

Forearm

**Correct Lines
AB equal to BC
AB parallel to BC**

Hock

Profile drawing of Belgian Sheepdog, showing correct conformation.

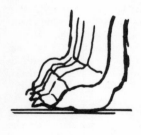

Cat-foot—correct on Belgian Sheepdog. Deep, short, round, compact foot. Short third digits bring toes closer to heel pad.

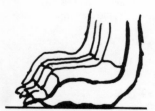

Hare-foot—faulty on Belgian Sheepdog. Longer third digits result in elongated foot.

Faulty undershot bite. Front teeth of lower jaw projecting beyond front teeth of upper jaw when mouth is closed.

Faulty overshot bite. Front teeth of upper jaw overlap and do not touch front teeth of lower jaw when mouth is closed.

12

Analysis of the Standard

The Standard, as it appears in *The Complete Dog Book*, published by the AKC, is primarily for judges. It must be concise and to the point. It is a guide only, for people to use in evaluating their dogs. The owner of a dog should read and study the breed Standard to know the desired qualities of his breed. However, it is impossible to know and understand the qualities of an outstanding specimen just by reading the Standard. It takes time, experience, the observation of many dogs, and studying dogs in general, to know what makes a champion.

The first thing to remember is that a dog is a complete unit. Each part of the body has a bearing on the function of another part of the body. When one part is not capable of completing its function in this complicated assembly of bones and muscles, then that part will become over-stressed. Nature will try to compensate by building up the muscle to the point where the dog will become unbalanced, and deterioration will be the final result.

Personality

The Belgian Sheepdog should be endowed with the qualities of intelligence, courage, and alertness that are necessary for the purpose for which the breed is intended. Originally, Belgian Sheepdogs were bred to be guardians of flocks of sheep, as well as to be protective of their homes and families. A dog is influenced by inherited traits as well as by environment. Good breeding and reliable ancestors are essential, but people must contribute to the development of their dog's personality with love, attention, basic training, and discipline in order to achieve the desired results. If the ancestors shown in your dog's pedigree are unstable, then there is a good chance that you will have the same type of dog, regardless of how much effort you put forth.

A dog should not show fear or shyness; he should be observant and vigilant with strangers, but not appre-hensive. With those he knows well, he should be affectionate and friendly.

Belgians are a spirited breed, yet they are sensitive and respond well to commands. They adapt well to training but do not respond well to rough treatment. If they understand what is expected of them they are willing and eager to please.

General Appearance

The Belgian Sheepdog should be a well balanced, medium size, square dog, elegant in appearance, with a proud carriage of head and neck. He is supposed to be strong, agile, well muscled, alert, and full of life. He should have solidity without bulkiness. Since the breed is well known for its agility and for being able to make quick turns (which are necessary in herding), the breeding of larger dogs would defeat the purpose for which the breed is intended. The breeding of small specimens that have fragile bone structure and no substance should also be discouraged. Any extreme deviation from medium size is a fault.

Coat

The guard hairs of the coat must be long, well fitting, straight, and abundant. They should not be silky or wiry. The texture should be of medium harshness. This is the desired coat, although the texture can vary according to the climate in which the dogs are raised. Dogs raised in mild, warm climates will not carry the same coat as dogs raised in cold climates. Dogs that live outside will grow coats to protect themselves from the elements, and the undercoat will be more dense. The guard hairs will be of a harder texture, for protection in rain and snow. Belgians will sometimes curl up in snow to sleep and practically become covered with snow, but if you examine the undercoat you will notice it is not wet.

It is not advisable for a dog that has spent most of his time in the house suddenly to be made to spend much time outside, for nature will not have had a chance to provide the proper insulation.

Color

Black dogs have a common problem. Since Belgians are working dogs and spend most of their time outside, they can, and many do, have a tendency to get sunburned in the heat of summer. A reddish cast to the coat is not uncommon. This condition is seasonal and should not be confused with poor pigmentation. Shedding and dead hair also detract from appearance.

Head

The head is the first thing you notice and remember about a dog. The size of the head and the expression of the face, the set of the ears, all should blend to form a pleasing picture. The head can also give you a good insight into the temperament and personality of the dog, but good head qualities are of far more importance to the body than just beauty, for muscles in the head, even though unseen, also affect the gait.

The skull is flattened rather than round. The width is approximately the same as but not greater than the length. The stop is moderate. The muzzle is moderately pointed, with no tendency to snipiness, and approximately equal in length to the skull.

The ears should be proportional in size to the head and body. The ears should be triangular in shape, stiff, and erect. The base of the ear should not come below the center of the eye. Belgians are noted for their small ears, and long ears can create problems. Sometimes the texture of the ear is too thin and soft to support the weight and the ears will fail to become erect. This usually is an inherited trait. Weak head muscles, improper ear set, or injured cartilage can contribute to this problem.

The ears are a dog's greatest asset. It is said that the human ear can hear sounds ranging between 1,500 and 15,000 vibrations per second. The dog's ear can hear sounds that range above 20,000. This is why dogs can hear higher-pitched sounds than humans can, and they can detect sounds which alert them to danger before the human ear can pick up the same sound. This is a great asset for herding or guard work, alerting dogs to danger to their charges which might go undetected if wind conditions prevented detection by their sense of smell.

Eyes

The Belgian Sheepdog Standard calls for brown eyes, preferably dark brown, of medium size, slightly almond shaped, and not protruding. There are no statistics that indicate a dark-eyed dog can see any better than one with a light eye. The color choice may have its origin in the idea of reflecting light. In reference to the color of the eye, we refer to the color of the iris, for the pupil is always black and it is the pupil and not the iris that reflects the light.

Many people think that a light-eyed dog, in a breed that is supposed to have dark eyes, is not as stable in temperament as the dark-eyed dog. The light eye is more noticeable in a black dog because the contrast between the eyes and the black coat gives the dog a more piercing stare and not the soft, friendly look that is characteristic of the Belgian Sheepdog.

Teeth

Needless to say, a full set of teeth—twenty upper, twenty-two lower—is to be desired. Belgians can have either an even or a scissor bite. If the incisors meet squarely, one above the other, the dog has a level or even bite. When the incisors slide past one another, the outside face of the lower just grazing the inside face of the upper, the dog has a scissor bite.

The even bite has many advantages for dogs that herd sheep. The dogs can and will pinch or nip the sheep and the even bite is not as destructive as the scissor bite when the dogs have to use force in directing the sheep. The scissor bite has its advantage in police work, because it gives the dogs a more secure grip. The scissor bite is easier on the teeth, for they do not wear down as fast as in the even bite, in which the teeth hit together directly every time.

Many people are confused about overshot and undershot bites. The overshot mouth has the upper incisor striking in front of the lower, while the undershot mouth has the lower striking in front of the upper.

Torso

The torso starts with the neck, and the Standard calls for a well-muscled neck. Since the head is important to the neck we cannot talk about one without also discussing the muscles necessary for locomotion. The head contains many muscles, such as those that raise or retract the ears, and the muscles that govern the eyes, but there are two muscles that are most important as far as function is concerned. The major one, *masseter*, is fastened to the lower jaw, just in front of the socket and the upper skull, and just above the back teeth, where it spreads out in a fan shape. It has more power than any other head muscle and is the biting muscle. The other important muscle, *zygomaticus*, is a long strip that extends from the cartilage of the ear in front of the lower jaw. It causes the jaw to retract.

There is also a cervical ligament that has flexible stretch and retraction. This ligament supports the neck and governs head carriage, and stabilizes the base attachment of the muscles that move the leg forward and rotate the shoulder blade as the leg moves backward. This ligament has two parts: the first cord runs along the top of the ligament from the base of the skull back to the fourth vertebra, where it becomes part of the spinal ligament; the second part is like a web running back from all the neck vertebrae, except two. This is the reason a well-muscled neck is so important: to complete its function as far as movement is concerned.

The head and neck of a dog have another very important function. Together they shift the center of gravity from side to side and help maintain equilibrium. When a dog is running he extends his neck and head forward, putting more weight forward, and increases his speed. When a dog comes to an abrupt stop from a high speed he will throw his head and neck high. This shifts the center of gravity backward and serves as a braking action. If the dog stopped abruptly with his head low and forward, he would probably fall.

The vertebral column is divided into five sections: neck, withers, back, croup, and tail.

The withers are slightly higher than the neck, and slope into the back, which must be level, straight, and firm from withers to hip joints. There are seven vertebrae in the neck. The first two differ in shape from the others and allow the head to move freely. The next five divide the neck into two parts, with separate sets of muscles attached to each part. This is the "pole" or arch in the back of the neck. This is functional and also gives the dog the proud carriage which we admire so much.

There are thirteen vertebrae (dorsal) that make up the withers and the back. The eight that compose the withers have the longest vertical spires and provide anchorage for the shoulder muscles. The five vertebrae that make up the back gradually change in shape from those of the withers to those of the loin (lumbar). There are seven vertebrae in the loin, and these have transverse prongs. The croup has three vertebrae (sacral) which are fused together for firmer anchorage to the pelvis. The number of vertebrae in the tail varies.

The back must be level, straight, and firm, since the power of the hindquarters must travel to the forequarters through the spinal column. Power can be transmitted faster and more forcefully in a straight line than through a convex curvature of the back (which is known as a roach back), or through a concave curvature of the back line between the withers and the hipbones (commonly called a swayback). The concave curvature usually occurs as a result of a combination of bad formation of the withers, a long back, and weak ligaments, and diminishes the dog's endurance and speed.

The back is a very important part which connects the fore and aft of the dog much like a bridge over which forward movements are conveyed from behind. It must be strong, with thick, hard, conditioned muscles, since it does a double duty of connecting and carrying, and works as the medium of transmitting power.

The Loin

The loin is one of the most misunderstood parts of a dog, but is a very important factor in performance. The loin is located between the rib section and the croup. There are seven vertebrae that control it. These are wider than the dorsal vertebrae, and their spinous processes, or fingers, are short, thin, and wide. The spinous processes incline forward to give better support to the rearing muscles. Their pull is backward, just the opposite of those in the shoulder. The loin does not have support from other bones of the frame, but is more like a bridge between two working parts of the dog's body.

Most Standards call for a slightly arched loin (for strength), since this section has little support other than muscles. This slight arch must not be confused with a roach back, which will draw the loin up. The loin section is relatively short, broad, and strong, but blends smoothly into the back. The loin must be long enough for flexibility but short enough for strength. This is achieved by depth. The girth of the loin is the result of solid, hard muscles, which are so important to the support of this section. Short but strong loins are essential for endurance. Too long a loin can be compared to a long span of a bridge without proper support.

The croup is a continuation of the back and should be of medium length, sloping gradually. This sounds simple enough, but these few words hold a great impact on the function of the rear end of a dog and in the action of the hind legs. A gradual slope from the pelvic bone to the set-on of the tail is to be desired. A dog with a level croup which is too short has a tendency to carry his tail high in the air. The dog will lack steadiness and the hindquarters will step short, with lack of thrust, which will restrict the gait. A dog that has a steep croup is hampered in his stride and lacks balance. The motion of the hind legs as the dog begins moving is more upward than forward. The transference of the motion through the back is interrupted, and the poor follow-through detracts from the smoothness and power of motion. A correctly formed croup will influence the proper carriage of the tail.

Chest

The chest is not broad, but deep. The lowest point should reach the elbow, forming a smooth ascendant curve to the abdomen.

The thorax should be capacious with plenty of room for heart and lungs. This must be achieved by a wide spring of rib at the junction of rib and spine, followed by an abrupt drop of the rib. This leaves the side of the dog flat, and offers a maximum of capacity with the least impediment to the action of the shoulder and legs.

Pose your dog in the correct position, place your hand slightly behind the elbow, and see for yourself if it is flat enough for the elbow to pass in a straight line. If there is a bulge and the leg is too tight against the body, you can be

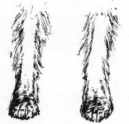

Good feet, with compact toes, well arched and muscular.

Weak, flat feet, with elongated toes and thin pads.

Splayed feet, lacking compactness and strength and easily injured. Feet are spread wide apart, with little or no arch.

Good conformation. Compact feet with pasterns slightly bent to absorb shock.

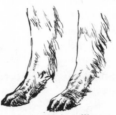

Weak pasterns which will not support weight of shoulder assembly, putting stress on leg muscles and tendons on back of leg.

Straight pasterns, indicating a straight shoulder assembly. Little or no shape to bones between pastern joint and foot.

East-west feet. Leg bones turned out. Weak ligaments. This is called "French standing," or "dancing master's position."

Fiddle front. Forelegs out at elbows, pasterns close, and feet turned out.

Toed-in stance. Toes turned in. Forelegs out at elbows. Elbows extended, protruding out from natural line of body from shoulder joint to foot when viewed from front. Breast too broad.

Narrow front, lacking depth of chest.

Front too wide.

Good front. Legs straight, strong, parallel to each other. Toes close knit, well arched, and compact.

16

sure there is not enough clearance there for the smooth passage of the leg.

There is a great difference between a well-sprung rib and a barrel-shaped rib. The barrel rib follows a circular line of the same relative degree from the spinal column to the junction with the brisket. The barrel-shaped ribs may look impressive but will cause the feet to toe in, with elbows out.

A small breast, without depth, will cause the front legs to draw in at the elbows, and the feet will turn out in an east-west position, which will prevent the feet and legs from traveling in a proper forward movement.

Forequarters

The forequarters develop no power of their own. Their main function is to lift the front and absorb the power transmitted from the hindquarters through the spinal column. Incorrect shoulders that do not permit the dog to reach far enough in front to keep the front feet out of the way of the hind feet will cause the dog to crab, or sidestep. The hind feet have to pass some way, and stepping to the side is the way of least resistance. A dog with a straight shoulder will not have an adequate length of neck. The proud arch of the neck will be lost and this will affect the gait, because a straight shoulder shifts the center of gravity and makes the maintenance of equilibrium difficult. If the shoulder does not allow sufficient reach to take care of the drive from the hindquarters, too much shock will be put on the front. Nature, in trying to compensate, will thicken the muscles, and the result will be loaded shoulders. When muscles thicken to gain strength the top is forced outward, bringing the shoulder point in and the elbows out. It is of little value to have well-angulated hindquarters to propel the animal without having sufficient angle of shoulder to absorb the stride. A dog with straight shoulders usually has a mincing gait, or may raise its front feet higher in a hackney gait, which fools a lot of people. It may look like a spirited gait, but the dog is only trying to extend beyond its normal reach. This constant pounding will, in time, result in loaded shoulders. A dog that is balanced on both ends, even though the ends are not particularly good, will move better than one that is good on one end and bad on the other.

The length of the layback (the angle of the shoulder blade as compared with the vertical) determines the length of reach, and the dog cannot reach any further. The better the layback, the smoother a dog will run, with the least amount of effort.

Legs and Feet

Two very important parts of a dog are the legs and the feet. The legs are to be straight, strong, and parallel to each other. The bone is oval rather than round. Development (length and substance) should be well proportioned. Length and substance well proportioned to the size of the dog is most important. A dog that reaches maximum height with small frail legs will look, and is, out of balance. There must be balance regardless of height. A dog that is undersized, with heavy bone and short legs, will look cumbersome, and the movement will lack the light, springy action that is characteristic of the Belgian gait. An unbalanced condition is not only offensive to the eye but in turn affects all other working parts of the body. Without balance, other functional parts of the framework will be under stress and deterioration of these parts will affect the working ability of the dog.

The pastern (that is, the region of the foreleg between the "wrist" and the digits) should be of medium length, strong, and slightly sloped. The pasterns of a Belgian will not be sloped as much as those of a German Shepherd, but a Belgian with a good layback of shoulder will have slightly sloped pasterns. A dog with straight shoulders or a short upper arm will have pasterns that are straight up and down. A line starting from the center of the shoulder blade, vertical to the ground, should pass through the large pad of the foot. If the pasterns are weak this may not necessarily be true. When we talk about weak pasterns then we must also talk about bad feet; when we talk about bad feet we find weak pasterns. It is hard to say which comes first. The feet may hold up better if they have more support, or if the feet are good to begin with, then the pasterns may be able to stand constant strain. Which is to blame makes no difference, for the results will be the same: the dog will not have the endurance that is needed in a working dog.

The feet should be round (cat-footed), with the toes curved closely together and well padded. The thickness of the pads depends on inheritance to a certain degree, but the type of terrain that the dog is exposed to makes a great difference. The pads must be thick in order to cushion the shock of normal movement. Even a dog that has good, thick pads will develop sore, tender feet if he is exposed to rough terrain after spending his life on a nice smooth lawn or thick carpet. If a dog is to be used as a working dog he should have his feet conditioned on crushed rock, gravel, or some other hard surface before being worked on rough, uneven ground.

Thin pads will not hold up for long on a working dog. Conditioning will help, but not much. Elongated toes are a serious problem. There is no way to develop a cat-foot from a foot with elongated toes. Proper terrain helps some, but the length of the toes is still there and the dog is going

Good hocks, broad and deep. Firm and well molded, never spongy or weak.

Hocks too close and too long. Weak.

Cow hocks, pointing inward toward one another. Leg action is on bias and loses efficiency.

Bandy legs or bowlegs.

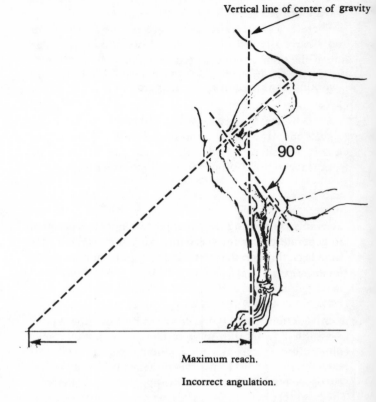

Vertical line of center of gravity

90°

Maximum reach.

Incorrect angulation.

Vertical line of center of gravity.

120°

Maximum reach.

Correct angulation.

Coming.

Going away.

Correct single tracking. Note that support leg is placed directly under center line of gravity.

to have splayed feet. Too little emphasis has been put on the elimination of poor feet. Since the feet support the entire dog when he is moving or standing still, eliminating poor feet should be an important factor in a breeding program. Compact feet add to the overall appearance of a dog, besides being less subject to injury when the dog is working or just running in the yard.

Hindquarters

The hindquarters play a different part than the forequarters. The muscles have of necessity to be broad and heavy in order to give the thrust that transmits the power through the back to the forequarters. The hind assembly is not designed to support weight. It is designed to generate power for speed and normal movement. The hind legs, through the stretching of muscles and the thrust from the ground, give the body forward momentum which is transferred to the forequarters through the back; this is called the "follow-through."

The hind legs are made up of many parts which affect the gait. They are composed of the upper part of the thigh joined to the pelvis, the second thigh, and the metatarsus joined with the hind feet. The skeleton is made up of the pelvic bones joined with the hip joint, the femur, the tibia and the fibula, and the bones of the hock, under which there are the powerful bones of the metatarsus and toes.

The pelvis provides an attachment for a large number of muscles which are important for motion. The power of its construction and the correctness of its position are of great importance to the efficiency of the dog. The gradual slope of the croup from the pelvic bones to the set-on of the tail is important to the hindquarters assembly. The correct position and good length of the femurs help complete the construction. The size and formation of the head or ball of the femur play an important role in smooth action. A deep socket with a well-formed head is a necessity. A malformed head or too shallow a socket is a characteristic of the dreaded hip dysplasia that plagues so many breeds. Also, a socket that is too deep, so that the head cannot move freely, will cause a restricted gait. This condition is like a piece of machinery where a joint or socket is so tight that it cannot move in rhythm with other mechanical parts, which in turn causes a breakdown in other parts that would perform normally if the timing was right.

It is easy to understand how a shallow socket, one that does not have the depth to let the femoral head rotate without slipping out, can cause constant damage not only to the head but to the inadequate socket as well. The gristle-like capsule that surrounds this area thickens to hold the femur in place. The femur head moves farther from the hip socket, becoming more deformed. Nature, in trying to compensate, builds up calcium deposits which in time cause the area to become inflamed and painful. This will lead to an arthritic condition, and it will be difficult for the dog to get up and down.

The Standard states that Belgians do not have *extreme* angulation, which is true, since they are supposed to resemble a square, but this does not mean that they do not have to have *good* angulation. In order to move forward at any speed that is required, they must have thrust from the hind legs to transmit power through the back to the forequarters. The bone extending from the hock joint should be broad and deep, indicating great strength. From the hock joint to the foot is the metatarsus. It should be short. If the metatarsus is too long the dog will lack endurance and quickness of movement.

The hind feet have the same requirements as the front feet but the hind feet must be proportionately stronger and longer, because their function is to impart a powerful push to the body. Dewclaws, which sometimes occur on the lower third of the inner part of the metatarsus, will interfere with stance and gait because the feet will have to adopt a wide stance, and a wide gait in order to miss the dewclaws. This is most noticeable when a dog is single-tracking. Dewclaws should be removed at an early age, when they are only loose excrescences with a nail, and only in rare cases joined to the bone by cartilagenous tissues. If left until maturity they not only hamper gait but are easily torn on rocks and rough ground.

Gait

When we talk about the proper functions of the different parts of a dog we are actually talking about how the parts affect the gait of the dog. A dog that is built properly should move well, but that does not always hold true because of the condition of the muscles. The dog must have exercise to strengthen the muscles and to achieve his potential. Muscles provide the power and force that make motion possible. Muscles are made up of fleshy elastic bands and nerve tissue. They lengthen and contract to move the bones to which they are attached. Each portion of the body has its own particular muscles that perform in unison with other sets of muscles to propel the dog forward.

First, we should understand a little about what happens in different types of gait. The *stride* is the distance traveled from one paw mark to the next by the same pad. *Timing* refers to the number of changes which take place in support of the body through the legs. *Right and left diagonal* describes the support when one front foot and the opposite back foot move together. This applies to either the right or left foot, whichever moves first.

The *walk* is a four-time movement, in which all four legs

move one after another. This gives four different combinations of weight support. Usually at least two, if not three, legs support the body at all times. As a general rule, the dog will lead off with the front foot. This permits the front foot to act a split second ahead of the back and will give clearance for the back foot; otherwise the dog will have to sidestep to miss the front foot. If he starts with the left front foot he will follow with the right rear foot, and vice-versa.

The *trot* shows the faults and good points of a dog better than any other gait. The trot is a two-time gait and brings into play the front and rear legs moving in unison with each other. To have proper support, the front foot will move slightly in advance of the corresponding back foot and will leave room for the back foot to advance. Watch the withers when a dog is in a trot. The withers should not bounce. Dogs seldom walk but usually are in either a slow trot or a fast trot. This gait is more suited to different types of terrain and provides greater endurance when traveling long distances.

The *pace* is a "fatigue" gait, and one to avoid in the show ring. The pace is a two-time lateral gait. The left front leg and the left rear leg move in unison, as do the right legs. This makes a shift of laterals from one side to another. This is an easy gait and less tiresome than the trot, and when a dog is tired he will resort to this gait in order to ease the toll of fatigue. Since this gait is a shifting from one side to the other it tends to ease the shock on the forequarters as the hindquarters help support the weight, but at the same time it gives a swing to the body, which helps as far as shock absorption is concerned, although the shifting motion is not pleasing to the eye. A dog is in the show ring for such a short time that he should not have to resort to the fatigue gait; if he does, there is something wrong, either in his physical construction or in his condition. Sometimes the handler moves in an in-between stride himself and forces the dog to match his stride.

The *gallop* is a gait that a dog uses when he has a need for increased speed. The major muscles which draw the rear legs backward are on the back side of the thigh. These muscles are commonly referred to as the rearing muscles. The rearing muscles are the important tools in this gait. The thrust is the force that sends the body forward, and is taken up by the extended front legs. The weight of the whole body is carried by these muscles when they lift up the front part of the body. If we know what makes these sudden bursts of speed possible, and how important the hocks and the rearing muscles are, we can see the need for strong hindquarters and strong backs to maintain speed for as long as is necessary. This is especially important in Belgians or any working dogs used for herding. They must be able to hold their speed until their charges can be headed off, and still have some reserve to call on in case of another change in direction.

In a fast gait the Belgian Sheepdog will single track, meaning the legs both front and rear converge toward the center line of gravity of the dog. The backline should remain firm and level, parallel to the line of motion, with no crabbing. A dog in a fast gait cannot maintain his equilibrium unless his legs converge toward the center line of gravity. This is the only way he can move in a straight line to prevent the sway of the body from side to side.

All herding dogs will single track in a fast gait, for they can then cover more ground with the least amount of effort. Even people single track when they walk or run. If you are in doubt about the mechanics of single tracking, go out in the yard and run in the normal manner, and watch your feet come in toward the center of gravity. Then place your feet about twelve inches apart, and go forward with your feet moving in a straight line. You can feel the pounding motion and your body will sway from side to side. It is easy to see why you could not run very far and maintain speed without physical exhaustion.

Faults

Any deviation from the Standard is classified as a fault. The extent to which any deviation affects the working ability of the dog determines whether the fault is considered major or minor.

Breeders must know the Standard and understand the function of all parts of the body in order to know to what extent their dogs deviate from the Standard. Even if a dog never does a day's work in his life, he still has to move. If he is put together right he will live his life with a minimum of body stress. A good example is the Veteran Class in a Specialty show. We see dogs moving with great ease at the age of twelve years, and older. These dogs were built right. Bad qualities as well as good qualities are going to affect the breed and the ability of future generations to function properly. Dog breeding is a responsibility that should not be taken lightly, if you love your breed.

Left to right: Ch. les Tsona de Jez Lancaster, Am. and Can. C.D.X.; Kathryn Courter; David Courter; and Ike V. Siegestor. Both dogs owned by Mary Courter.

Glossary of Terms Relating to Conformation

Almond eyes—The set of the eye is almond shaped rather than round.

Apple head—Rounded topskull, more humped toward the center.

Butterfly nose—Parti-color nose, dark with flesh colored markings.

Crabbing—A side-wise movement of the body at an angle to the line of progress.

Dew claws—Extra claw or functionless fifth toe on inside of leg.

Flat croup—Croup with little or no slope downward from the back line.

Flat-sided—Ribs relatively flat in mid-section.

Frog-face—Extended nose with receding jaw, usually over-shot.

Gay tail—Tail carried high above the back line.

Goose rump—Too steep or sloping croup.

Hackney action—The high lifting of the front feet as in a hackney horse.

Layback—The angle of the shoulder blade.

Lippy—Loose lips that do not fit tightly.

Loaded shoulders—Shoulder blades under which the muscles have been over-developed so blades push outward from the body.

Loin—The region of the body on both sides of the vertebral column between the lower ribs and the hindquarters.

Out at elbows—Elbows protruding from natural line of the body when viewed from the front.

Out at shoulder—Blade-set that places the joints too far apart for proper movement.

Pigeon-breast—Chest with protruding breastbone.

Roach-back—Pronounced convex curve of back line toward loin. (Sometimes called carp back.)

Shelly—Shallow, narrow body, very little spring to ribs.

Sickle hocked—In a standing position the hock joint is bent at an angle rather than vertical to the ground, resembling a sickle.

Sickle tail—Tail carried high in a semi-circle.

Snipey face—Pointed weak muzzle lacking in bone formation.

Spring of ribs—Curve of ribs for lung and heart capacity.

Sway-back—Concave curve in back line between withers and hipbones.

Undershot—Front teeth of lower jaw projecting beyond front teeth of upper jaw when mouth is closed.

Wry mouth—Lower jaw is not aligned with upper jaw.

Weaving—Crossing of forefeet or hind feet when in motion.

Ch. High Mount's Coup de Grace, BOS at the 1983 BSCA National Specialty. Owner, Linda McCarty. Photo by John Ashbey.

Grooming the Belgian Sheepdog

Equipment

Grooming requires proper tools and a grooming table with an adjustable arm for securing the dog's head, or a crate with a grooming table top. Rubber matting provides a non-slip surface. It is important to have a sturdy table or crate that will not wobble and create a sense of insecurity. It is best to start out with short grooming sessions until the dog becomes adjusted to the routine. After a few sessions the dog will look forward to the additional attention and to your personal touch.

The tools are a matter of choice and depend on the condition of the coat. I prefer a wire brush with teeth about an inch long, a good, natural bristle brush, a comb with medium-spaced teeth, nail clippers, a file, a pair of surgical-type scissors with blunt points, and thinning scissors.

The Coat

Grooming a Belgian can be as complicated or as simple as you want to make it. Much will depend on your regular grooming habits and on the terrain in which your dog spends most of his time. A house dog that runs on a well-kept lawn will require less time to groom than a dog that runs and works in weeds and high grass. Burs, seeds, and grass can become embedded in the coat, and the longer they are neglected the longer it will take to work them out without damage to the coat and discomfort to the dog. They can cause skin irritation, which can result in open lesions due to scratching.

The Belgian Sheepdog grows a coat according to his need for protection from the elements. The outer coat provides protection from rain and snow and the undercoat provides insulation against heat and cold. Shedding usually starts with warm weather. The undercoat will start to loosen and come out gradually, and must be removed to prevent matting and discomfort to the dog. A short, daily brushing session will remove loose hair. Brushing will not be a major project unless you wait until an accumulation of dead hair has started to mat and tangle.

When you are ready to do a thorough job of grooming, put your dog on the grooming table or crate. Secure the dog's head to the grooming post or have someone hold the head to prevent the dog from moving around. Everyone has his own procedure, and it makes no difference as long as the result is satisfactory.

Massage the body and skin with your fingers and stir up the hair. This will loosen dandruff, caused by dryness, and will stimulate circulation as well as secretion of the skin's natural oils. Take a natural bristle brush and brush against the grain from the rear toward the head. While you are doing this, check for fleas and ticks or skin abrasions. Then brush from the head towards the tail. This will help loosen dead hair which can be removed with a comb or wire brush. When you have finished with the removal of dead hair, again use the bristle brush to brush the coat forward toward the head, let the dog shake himself, and the hair will fall in its natural place.

The hocks may have excessive hair on the back side, and this should be trimmed with thinning scissors, which have teeth that create a much neater appearance than the cut of regular scissors. The metatarsus, or what we commonly call the hock, should have a straight, clean look.

Excess hair also grows on the back of the front pasterns. This hair, a short distance above the foot, should be removed with thinning scissors. Trim the hair around the foot to give a rounded appearance. Pull excess hair between the toes upward with your fingers and remove with blunt scissors.

Sometimes hair along the loin area will grow in different lengths and detract from the contour of the body. This hair should be trimmed with thinning scissors to eliminate the uneven look.

If you are going to show the dog, grooming should be done at least a week before a show.

Toenails

Check the nails, for they may need a little trimming. Snip a small amount from the tip to avoid cutting the blood vessels in the nail, and then file the nail. Draw the file in only one direction. A downward stroke will give a more finished look. Long nails will cause an unnatural stance that can in turn cause lameness and splay the toes. Do not overlook the dewclaws on the front legs. They curl under as they grow, sometimes even circling back and piercing the skin. If you have let the nails get too long, it may be easier to take the dog to your veterinarian and have him trim them. Once the nails are cut back, a few strokes with a file every week should keep them at a proper length.

Right, Ch. Laralee's Rebel Roc O'Lorahame, C.D.X., Sch-H I. (Ch. Laralee's Rebel x Ch. Mi-Sha-Ook's Legacy, C.D.) Owner, Freya Robison.

Left, Ch. Touraline's Famous Amos, BOS at the 1982 BSCA National Specialty. Owners, Laura and Wayne Bellows.

Right, the first Mexican and American Tracking Dog title winners: Left, Mex. and Am. Ch. Condor V. Siegestor, U.D.T., P.C., E.T., Mex. T.D., A.T.D., Int. Sch-H III. Owner, Kathy Marti. Right, Ch. Bando V. Siegestor, C.D., Am. and Mex. T.D., E.T., A.T.D. Owners, Mara Lee Jiles and Rayeann Schur.

Eyes, Ears, and Teeth

Mucus can collect in the corners of your dog's eyes. Wipe the eyes with a piece of cotton or a soft tissue, being careful not to touch the eyeball and cause irritation. If there is a definite discharge, you should check with your veterinarian. If there is any redness in the eye, you can use an ophthalmic ointment to soothe and clear the eye. If redness continues, it may be the result of a foreign object in the eye, in which case the eye needs to be flushed. Some people use a mild boric acid solution for this.

Check your dog's ears often. You can remove dirt and wax from the folds of the upper ear with a swab dipped in a mild solution of boric acid, or you can wrap some cotton that has been dampened with witch hazel around your forefinger and clean only what you can see. Do not probe in the ear canal. If your dog constantly shakes his head, twitches, or scratches at his ear, a seed or some other foreign object may have gotten in the ear canal. If this is the case, it should be removed by a veterinarian with an ear speculum. Internal ear canker can cause the same symptoms. Ear mites are another problem that can cause great discomfort to a dog. In all cases of ear disease, your veterinarian's services should be obtained at once, for a delay may result in a chronic, and sometimes incurable, condition.

Cleaning a dog's teeth can be a problem if the dog is not introduced to the procedure at an early age. Most dogs resist examination of the teeth. The dog in his natural state, may keep his teeth in good condition, but through years of domesticity, the dog, like ourselves, suffers from tooth decay and tartar deposits. Tartar accumulates when a dog eats soft food over too long a period of time. If it accumulates in large quantities, it pushes back the gums, exposing the roots of the teeth, which will become loosened. Decomposed foods become lodged in the cavities, with the result being that pyorrhea may develop, along with irritation. In an older dog's teeth, abscesses occur frequently at the base of the root system. This usually occurs when the dog has not had proper tooth care.

Some people brush their dog's teeth with a solution of table salt. Giving the dog a large knuckle bone that will not splinter helps keep tartar from accumulating. Hard dog biscuits are good for the teeth as well as being a pleasant treat. If a large quantity of tartar is present on the teeth, the dog should be taken to a veterinarian, who will anesthetize the gums to remove the tartar and prevent suffering. An ounce of prevention is worth a pound of cure, so start early and don't neglect the teeth.

Bathing

A normal, healthy dog should not be bathed frequently. A Belgian Sheepdog's skin is rich in oil glands and deficient in sweat glands. The natural oil will prevent the skin from becoming dry and will help to keep the coat water resistant. If you bathe the dog too often, this natural oil is removed and the skin can become irritated. The dog may scratch and bite himself, and this can cause open abrasions which can be slow to heal. A well-groomed Belgian does not have a doggy odor, but occasionally he will have to have a bath if he has been in mud or has rolled in some offensive substance that cannot be removed with a brush. If you do not have a kennel room and tub, you can put a non-slip mat in your bathtub. To avoid getting the floor wet, spread newspaper on the floor in front of the tub, then plug the dog's ears with cotton to prevent water from getting in the ear canal. To protect the eyes, some people use a drop of castor oil, or you can use your ophthalmic ointment, which is soothing as well as protective. There are numerous soaps and shampoos on the market, and they all have their good and bad qualities. Some of these soaps contain carbolic acid and bichloride of mercury. These soaps, though they kill fleas, sometimes cause eczema, which is quite difficult to cure. A mild shampoo, even some of your own, will do a good job. The water should be tepid, never too hot or too cold. Work the shampoo well into the coat and then rinse every trace of shampoo from the coat. The head should be washed last. Using a washcloth is the easiest way to clean the head and to avoid getting shampoo in the dog's eyes.

When a dog comes out of a bath he will shake himself, and that is when you get an extra bath if you are not careful. Drop a large towel over his back and let him shake the excess water from his coat, and then rub him vigorously until he is dry. If the weather is warm, he can be let outside to finish drying, but if it is cold he should be kept inside until he is thoroughly dry. In hot weather you can put a drop cloth on the ground and bathe your dog outside, using your garden hose. It works just as well and saves a lot of work cleaning up after an indoor bath.

If you are going to show your dog, a bath should be given a few days before the show to allow the natural oils to return to the coat. Brushing will help restore the oil in the coat and give a nice sheen.

Trimming the whiskers of a dog is a matter of choice. Most people who show their dogs do trim the whiskers to give a clean look to the muzzle. If you do not intend to show your dog, this is not necessary.

Above, Ch. Endymion's Charisma, C.D. Owner, Linda McCarty.

Above, Ch. Bando V. Siegestor, C.D., T.D., E.T., A.T.D., and Ch. Esprit De Noir V. Siegestor, C.D.X., E.T., Sch-H I. Owners, Rayeann Schur and Mara Lee Jiles.

Above, Ch. Belle Noire Torreson. (Ch. Charro of Geier Tal x Ch. Van Mell's Dynasty, C.D.) Owners, Marge and Ed Turnquist.

Right, Ch. Voudouns's Rowdy Wolf, C.D. Owners, Margery and Jon Riddle.

"Bed and Board" for the Family Dog

It is much easier to adapt to the demands of a new puppy if you collect the necessary equipment before you bring him home. You will need a water and food dish—preferably stainless steel and of a type that will not tip easily. You will need some chew toys, a soft puppy lead, and a soft hair brush for puppy grooming. You will need to decide where your dog is going to sleep and to prepare his bed.

Every dog should have a bed of his own, snug and warm, where he can retire undisturbed when he wishes to nap. And, especially with a small puppy, it is desirable to have the bed arranged so the dog can be securely confined at times, safe and contented. If the puppy is taught early in life to stay quietly in his box at night, or when the family is out, the habit will carry over into adulthood and will benefit both dog and master.

The dog should never be banished to a damp, cold basement, but should be quartered in an out-of-the-way corner close to the center of family activity. His bed can be an elaborate cushioned affair with electric warming pad, or simply a rectangular wooden box or heavy paper carton, cushioned with a clean cotton rug or towel. Actually, the latter is ideal for a new puppy, for it is snug, easy to clean, and expendable. A "door" can be cut on one side of the box for easy access, but it should be placed in such a way that the dog can still be confined when desirable.

The shipping crates used by professional handlers at dog shows make ideal indoor quarters. They are lightweight but strong, provide adequate air circulation, yet are snug and warm and easily cleaned. For the dog owner who takes his dog along when he travels, a dog crate is ideal, for the dog will willingly stay in his accustomed bed during long automobile trips, and the crate can be taken inside motels or hotels at night, making the dog a far more acceptable guest.

Dog crates are made of chromed metal or wood, and some have tops covered with a special rubber matting so they can be used as grooming tables. Anyone moderately handy with tools can construct a crate similar to the type available from pet supply dealers.

Crates come in various sizes, to suit various breeds of dogs. For reasons of economy, the size selected for a puppy should be adequate for use when the dog is full grown. If the area seems too large when the puppy is small, a temporary cardboard partition can be installed to limit the area he occupies.

For the owner's convenience and to enhance the dog's sense of security, food and water dishes may be kept in the same general area where the crate is kept.

Nutrition

The main food elements required by dogs are proteins, fats, and carbohydrates. Vitamins A, B complex, D, and E are essential, as are ample amounts of calcium and iron. Nine other minerals are required in small amounts but are amply provided in almost any diet, so there is no need to be concerned about them.

The most important nutrient is protein and it must be provided every day of the dog's life, for it is essential for normal daily growth and replacement of body tissues burned up in daily activity. Preferred animal protein products are beef, mutton, horse meat, and boned fish. Visceral organs—heart, liver, and tripe—are good but if used in too large quantities may cause diarrhea (bones in large amounts have the same effect). Some veterinarians feel that pork is undesirable, while others consider lean pork acceptable as long as it is well cooked. Bacon drippings are often recommended for inclusion in the dog's diet, but this is a matter best discussed with your veterinarian since the salt in the bacon drippings might prove harmful to a dog that is not in good health. The "meat meal" used in some commercial foods is made from scrap meat processed at high temperatures and then dried. It is not quite so nutritious as fresh meat, but in combination with other protein products, it is an acceptable ingredient in the dog's diet.

Cooked eggs and raw egg yolk are good sources of protein, but raw egg white should never be fed since it may cause diarrhea. Cottage cheese and milk (fresh, dried, and canned) are high in protein, also. Puppies thrive on milk and it is usually included in the diet until the puppy is about three months of age, but when fed to older dogs it often causes diarrhea. Soy-bean meal, wheat germ meal, and dried brewers yeast are vegetable products high in protein and may be used to advantage in the dog's diet.

Vegetable and animal fats in moderate amounts should be used, especially if a main ingredient of the diet is dry or kibbled food. Fats should not be used excessively or the dog may become overweight. Generally, fats should be increased slightly in the winter and reduced somewhat during warm weather.

Carbohydrates are required for proper assimilation of fats. Dog biscuits, kibble, dog meal, and other dehydrated foods are good sources of carbohydrates, as are cereal products derived from rice, corn, wheat, and oats.

Vegetables supply additional proteins, vitamins, and minerals, and by providing bulk are of value in overcoming constipation. Raw or cooked carrots, celery, lettuce, beets, asparagus, tomatoes, and cooked spinach may be used. They should always be chopped or ground well and mixed with the other food. Various combinations may be used, but a good home-mixed ration for the mature dog consists of two parts of meat and one each of vegetables and dog meal (or cereal product).

27

Dicalcium phosphate and cod-liver oil are added to puppy diets to ensure inclusion of adequate amounts of calcium and Vitamins A and D. Indiscriminate use of dietary supplements is not only unjustified but may be harmful and many breeders feel that their over-use may lead to excessive growth as well as to overweight at maturity. Also, kidney damage in adult dogs has been traced to over-supplementation of the diet with calcium and Vitamin D.

Foods manufactured by well-known and reputable food processors are nutritionally sound and are offered in sufficient variety of flavors, textures, and consistencies that most dogs will find them tempting and satisfying. Canned foods are usually "ready to eat," while dehydrated foods in the form of kibble, meal, or biscuits may require the addition of water or milk. Dried foods containing fat sometimes become rancid, so to avoid an unpalatable change in flavor, the manufacturer may not include fat in dried food but recommend its addition at the time the water or milk is added.

Candy and other sweets are taboo, for the dog has no nutritional need for them and if he is permitted to eat them, he will usually eat less of foods he requires. Also taboo are fried foods, highly seasoned foods, and extremely starchy foods, for the dog's digestive tract is not equipped to handle them.

Frozen foods should be thawed completely and warmed at least to lukewarm, while hot foods should be cooled to lukewarm. Food should be in a fairly firm state, for sloppy food is difficult for the dog to digest.

Whether meat is raw or cooked makes little difference, so long as the dog is also given the juice that seeps from the meat during cooking. Bones provide little nourishment, although gnawing bones helps make the teeth strong and helps to keep tartar from accumulating on them. Beef bones, especially large knuckle bones, are best. Fish, poultry, and chop bones should never be given to dogs since they have a tendency to splinter and may puncture the dog's digestive tract.

Clean, fresh, cool water is essential and an adequate supply should be available twenty-four hours a day from the time the puppy is big enough to walk. Especially during hot weather, the drinking pan should be emptied and refilled at frequent intervals.

Puppies usually are weaned by the time they are six weeks old, so when you acquire a new puppy ten or twelve weeks old, he will already have been started on a feeding schedule. The breeder should supply exact details as to number of meals per day, types and amounts of food offered, etc. It is essential to adhere to this established routine, for drastic changes in diet may produce intestinal upsets. In most instances, a combination of dry meal,

Nutrient Requirements (and Selected Recommended Allowances) of Dogs
(percentage or amount per kilogram of food)

	Type of Diet				
	Dry Basis	Dry Type	Semimoist	Canned or Wet	
Moisture level (%)	0	10	25	75	
Dry matter basis (%)	100	90	75	25	
Nutrient	Requirement				Principal Function
Protein	22%	20%	16.5%	5.5%	Growth, maintenance
Fat	5.0%	4.5%	3.75%	1.25%	Energy, skin, coat
Linoleic acid	1.0%	0.9%	0.75%	0.25%	Skin, coat
Calcium	1.1%	1.0%	0.8%	0.3%	Skeletal structure, teeth
Phosphorus	0.9%	0.8%	0.7%	0.22%	Skeletal structure, teeth
Potassium	0.6%	0.5%	0.45%	0.2%	Muscles
Sodium chloride	1.1%	1.0%	0.8%	0.3%	Body fluids
Magnesium	0.040%	0.036%	0.030%	0.010%	Muscles, skeletal structure
Iron	60 mg	54 mg	45 mg	15 mg	Blood
Copper	7.3 mg	6.5 mg	5.5 mg	1.8 mg	Blood
Manganese	5.0 mg	4.5 mg	3.8 mg	1.2 mg	Metabolism
Zinc	50 mg	45 mg	38 mg	12 mg	Skin
Iodine	1.54 mg	1.39 mg	1.16 mg	0.39 mg	Thyroid
Selenium	0.11 mg	0.10 mg	0.08 mg	0.03 mg	Muscles
Vitamin A	5,000 IU	4,500 IU	3,750 IU	1,250 IU	Eyes, skin
Vitamin D	500 IU	450 IU	375 IU	125 IU	Skeletal structure, teeth
Vitamin E	50 IU	45 IU	37.5 IU	12.5 IU	Reproduction, muscles
Thiamin	1.00 mg	0.90 mg	0.75 mg	0.25 mg	Nerves, digestion
Riboflavin	2.2 mg	2.0 mg	1.6 mg	0.5 mg	Enzymes
Pantothenic acid	10.0 mg	9.0 mg	7.5 mg	2.5 mg	Growth
Niacin	11.4 mg	10.3 mg	8.6 mg	2.8 mg	Nerves
Pyridoxine	1.0 mg	0.9 mg	0.75 mg	0.25 mg	Blood, growth
Folic acid	0.18 mg	0.16 mg	0.14 mg	0.04 mg	Blood
Biotin	0.10 mg	0.09 mg	0.075 mg	0.025 mg	Skin, coat
Vitamin B$_{12}$	0.022 mg	0.020 mg	0.017 mg	0.006 mg	Blood
Choline	1,200 mg	1,100 mg	900 mg	300 mg	Liver, nerves

Nutrient data from **Nutrient Requirements for Dogs** (1974 Revision) published by National Research Council, National Academy of Sciences, Washington, D.C.

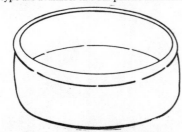

Dishes of this type are available in both plastic and stainless steel.

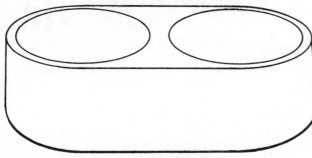

Crockery dish for food or water.

Stainless steel dish for food and water.

canned meat, and the plastic wrapped hamburger-like products provide a well-balanced diet. For a puppy that is too fat or too thin, or for one that has health problems, a veterinarian may recommend a specially formulated diet, but ordinarily, the commercially prepared foods can be used.

The amount of food offered at each meal must gradually be increased and by five months the puppy will require about twice what he needed at three months. However, the puppy should not be allowed to become too fat. Obesity has become a major health problem for dogs, and it is estimated that forty-one percent of American dogs are overweight. It is essential that weight be controlled throughout the dog's lifetime and that the dog be kept in trim condition—neither too fat nor too thin— for many physical problems can be traced directly to overweight. If the habit of overeating is developed in puppyhood, controlling the weight of the mature dog will be much more difficult.

A mature dog usually eats slightly less than he did as a growing puppy. For mature dogs, one large meal a day is usually sufficient, although some owners prefer to give two meals. As long as the dog enjoys optimum health and

is neither too fat nor too thin, the number of meals a day makes little difference.

The amount of food required for mature dogs will vary. With canned dog food or home-prepared foods (that is, the combination of meat, vegetables, and meal), the approximate amount required is one-half ounce of food per pound of body weight. If the dog is fed a dehydrated commercial food, approximately one ounce of food is needed for each pound of body weight. Most manufacturers of commercial foods provide information on packages as to approximate daily needs of various breeds.

For most dogs, the amount of food provided should be increased slightly during the winter months and reduced somewhat during hot weather when the dog is less active.

As a dog becomes older and less active, he may become too fat. Or his appetite may decrease so he becomes too thin. It is necessary to adjust the diet in either case, for the dog will live longer and enjoy better health if he is maintained in trim condition. The simplest way to decrease or increase body weight is by decreasing or increasing the amount of fat in the diet. Protein content should be maintained at a high level throughout the dog's life.

If the older dog becomes reluctant to eat, it may be necessary to coax him with special food he normally relishes. Warming the food will increase its aroma and usually will help to entice the dog to eat. If he still refuses, rubbing some of the food on the dog's lips and gums may stimulate interest. It may be helpful also to offer food in smaller amounts and increase the number of meals per day. Foods that are highly nutritious and easily digested are especially desirable for older dogs. Small amounts of cooked, ground liver, cottage cheese, or mashed, hard-cooked eggs should be included in the diet often.

Before a bitch is bred, her owner should make sure that she is in optimum condition—slightly on the lean side rather than fat. The bitch in whelp is given much the same diet she was fed prior to breeding, with slight increases in amounts of meat, liver, and dairy products. Beginning about six weeks after breeding, she should be fed two meals per day rather than one, and the total daily intake increased. (Some bitches in whelp require as much as 50% more food than they consumed normally.) She must not be permitted to become fat, for whelping problems are more likely to occur in overweight dogs. Cod-liver oil and dicalcium phosphate should be provided until after the puppies are weaned.

The dog used only occasionally for breeding will not require a special diet, but he should be well fed and maintained in optimum condition. A dog used frequently may require a slightly increased amount of food. But his basic diet will require no change so long as his general health is good and his flesh is firm and hard.

Ch. Belle Noir Granada. (Ch. Charro of Geier Tal x Ch. Van Mell's Dynasty, C.D.) Owner, Carolyn Hackney.

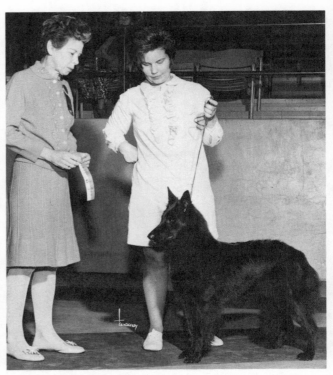

Ch. Vicci's Concertina. (Thunderstone's Frosty Night x Zenabeth of Geier Tal.) Owner, Carole Vander-Meulen.

Ch. Lorjen Spirit of Seventy-Six. (Ch. Solange On Stage O'Ebon Will x Ch. Stage Fire O'Ebon Will.) Judge, J. T. Gately. Handler, Joy Brewster. Owners, Roger and Maxine Ellis.

Ch. Jeamill's Gold Star of Ganymede, C.D. (Tom Collins of Ganymede x Ganymede of Black Mountain.) Judge, Robert Ward. Owners, Millard and Jeani Brown.

Maintaining the Dog's Health

In dealing with health problems, simple measures of preventive care are always preferable to cures—which may be complicated and costly. Many of the problems which afflict dogs can be avoided quite easily by instituting good dog-keeping practices in connection with feeding and housing.

Proper nutrition is essential in maintaining the dog's resistance to infectious disease, in reducing susceptibility to organic disease, and, of course, in preventing dietary deficiency diseases.

Cleanliness is essential in preventing the growth of disease-producing bacteria and other micro-organisms. All equipment, especially water and food dishes, must be kept immaculately clean. Cleanliness is also essential in controlling external parasites, which thrive in unsanitary surroundings.

Symptoms of Illness

Symptoms of illness may be so obvious there is no question that the dog is ill, or so subtle that the owner isn't sure whether there is a change from normal or not. **Loss of appetite, malaise** (general lack of interest in what is going on), **and vomiting** may be ignored if they occur singly and persist only for a day. However, in combination with other evidence of illness, such symptoms may be significant and the dog should be watched closely. **Abnormal bowel movements,** especially diarrhea or bloody stools, are causes for immediate concern. **Urinary abnormalities** may indicate infections, and bloody urine is always an indication of a serious condition. When a dog that has long been housebroken suddenly becomes incontinent, a veterinarian should be consulted, for he may be able to suggest treatment or medication that will be helpful.

Fever is a positive indication of illness and consistent deviation from the normal temperature range of 100 to 102 degrees is cause for concern. Have the dog in a standing position when taking his temperature. Coat the bulb of a rectal thermometer with petroleum jelly, raise the dog's tail, insert the thermometer to approximately half its length, and hold it in position for two minutes. Clean the thermometer with rubbing alcohol after each use and be sure to shake it down.

Fits, often considered a symptom of worms, may result from a variety of causes, including vitamin deficiencies, or playing to the point of exhaustion. A veterinarian should be consulted when a fit occurs, for it may be a symptom of serious illness.

Persistent coughing is often considered a symptom of worms, but may also indicate heart trouble—especially in older dogs.

Stary coat—dull and lackluster—indicates generally poor health and possible worm infestation. **Dull eyes** may result from similar conditions. Certain forms of blindness may also cause the eyes to lose the sparkle of vibrant good health.

Vomiting is another symptom often attributed to worm infestation. Dogs suffering from indigestion sometimes eat grass, apparently to induce vomiting and relieve discomfort.

Accidents and Injuries

Injuries of a serious nature—deep cuts, broken bones, severe burns, etc.—always require veterinary care. However, the dog may need first aid before being moved to a veterinary hospital.

A dog injured in any way should be approached cautiously, for reactions of a dog in pain are unpredictable and he may bite even a beloved master. A muzzle should always be applied before any attempt is made to move the dog or treat him in any way. The muzzle can be improvised from a strip of cloth, bandage, or even heavy cord, looped firmly around the dog's jaws and tied under the lower jaw. The ends should then be extended back of the neck and tied again so the loop around the jaws will stay in place.

A stretcher for moving a heavy dog can be improvised from a rug or board, and preferably two people should be available to transport it. A small dog can be carried by one person simply by grasping the loose skin at the nape of the neck with one hand and placing the other hand under the dog's hips.

Burns from chemicals should first be treated by flushing the coat with plain water, taking care to protect the dog's eyes and ears. A baking soda solution can then be applied to neutralize the chemical further. If the burned area is small, a bland ointment should be applied. If the burned area is large, more extensive treatment will be required, as well as veterinary care.

Burns from hot liquid or hot metals should be treated by applying a bland ointment, provided the burned area is small. Burns over large areas should be treated by a veterinarian.

Electric shock usually results because an owner negligently leaves an electric cord exposed where the dog can chew on it. If possible, disconnect the cord before touching the dog. Otherwise, yank the cord from the dog's mouth so you will not receive a shock when you try to help him. If the dog is unconscious, artificial respiration and stimulants will be required, so a veterinarian should be consulted at once.

Fractures require immediate professional attention. A broken bone should be immobilized while the dog is transported to the veterinarian but no attempt should be made to splint it.

Poisoning is more often accidental than deliberate, but whichever the case, symptoms and treatment are the same. If the poisoning is not discovered immediately, the dog may be found unconscious. His mouth will be slimy, he will tremble, have difficulty breathing, and possibly go into convulsions. Veterinary treatment must be secured immediately.

If you find the dog eating something you know to be poisonous, induce vomiting immediately by repeatedly forcing the dog to swallow a mixture of equal parts of hydrogen peroxide and water. Delay of even a few minutes may result in death. When the contents of the stomach have been emptied, force the dog to swallow raw egg white, which will slow absorption of the poison. Then call the veterinarian. Provide him with information as to the type of poison, and follow his advice as to further treatment.

Some chemicals are toxic even though not swallowed, so before using a product, make sure it can be used safely around pets.

Severe bleeding from a leg can be controlled by applying a tourniquet between the wound and the body, but the tourniquet must be loosened at ten-minute intervals. Severe bleeding from head or body can be controlled by placing a cloth or gauze pad over the wound, then applying firm pressure with the hand.

To treat minor cuts, first trim the hair from around the wound, then wash the area with warm soapy water and apply a mild antiseptic such as tincture of metaphen.

Shock is usually the aftermath of severe injury and requires immediate veterinary attention. The dog appears dazed, lips and tongue are pale, and breathing is shallow. The dog should be wrapped in blankets and kept warm, and if possible, kept lying down with his head lower than his body.

Bacterial and Viral Diseases

Distemper takes many and varied forms, so it is sometimes difficult for even experienced veterinarians to diagnose. It is the number one killer of dogs, and although it is not unknown in older dogs, its victims are usually puppies. While some dogs do recover, permanent damage to the brain or nervous system is often sustained. Symptoms may include lethargy, diarrhea, vomiting, reduced appetite, cough, nasal discharge, inflammation of the eyes, and a rise in temperature. If distemper is suspected, a veterinarian must be consulted at once, for early treatment is essential. Effective preventive measures lie in inoculation. Shots for temporary immunity should be given all puppies within a few weeks after whelping, and the permanent inoculations should be given as soon thereafter as possible.

Hardpad has been fairly prevalent in Great Britain for a number of years, and its incidence in the United States is increasing. Symptoms are similar to those of distemper, but as the disease progresses, the pads of the feet harden and eventually peel. Chances of recovery are not favorable unless prompt veterinary care is secured.

Infectious hepatitis in dogs affects the liver, as does the human form, but apparently is not transmissible to man. Symptoms are similar to those of distemper, and the disease rapidly reaches the acute state. Since hepatitis is often fatal, prompt veterinary treatment is essential. Effective vaccines are available and should be provided all puppies. A combination distemper-hepatitis vaccine is sometimes used.

Leptospirosis is caused by a micro-organism often transmitted by contact with rats, or by ingestion of food contaminated by rats. The disease can be transmitted to man, so anyone caring for an afflicted dog must take steps to avoid infection. Symptoms include vomiting, loss of appetite, diarrhea, fever, depression and lethargy, redness of eyes and gums, and sometimes jaundice. Since permanent kidney damage may result, veterinary treatment should be secured immediately.

Parvovirus is a highly contagious and often fatal intestinal disease characterized by severe vomiting and diarrhea (often bloody), a high temperature, and rapid dehydration. Although usually preceded by lethargy and loss of appetite, the onset is sudden, and veterinary treatment must be sought at the first sign of symptoms. A preventive vaccine affords protection but must, of course, be given before symptoms appear.

Rabies is a disease that is always fatal—and it is transmissible to man. It is caused by a virus that attacks the nervous system and is present in the saliva of an infected animal. When an infected animal bites another, the virus is transmitted to the new victim. It may also enter the body through cuts and scratches that come in contact with saliva containing the virus.

All warm-blooded animals are subject to rabies, and it may be transmitted by foxes, skunks, squirrels, horses, and cattle as well as dogs. Anyone bitten by a dog (or other animal) should see his physician immediately, and health and law enforcement officials should be notified. Also, if your dog is bitten by another animal, consult your veterinarian immediately.

In most areas, rabies shots are required by law. Even if not required, all dogs should be given anti-rabies vaccine, for it is an effective preventive measure.

Dietary Deficiency Diseases

Rickets afflicts puppies not provided sufficient calcium and Vitamin D. Symptoms include lameness, arching of neck and back, and a tendency of the legs to bow. Treatment consists of providing adequate amounts of dicalcium phosphate and Vitamin D and exposing the dog to sunlight. If detected and treated before reaching an advanced stage, bone damage may be lessened somewhat, although it cannot be corrected completely.

Osteomalacia, similar to rickets, may occur in adult dogs. Treatment is the same as for rickets, but here, too, prevention is preferable to cure. Permanent deformities resulting from rickets or osteomalacia will not be inherited, so once victims recover, they can be used for breeding.

External Parasites

Fleas, lice, mites, and ticks can be eradicated in the dog's quarters by regular use of one of the insecticide sprays with a four to six weeks' residual effect. Bedding, blankets, and pillows should be laundered frequently and treated with an insecticide. Treatment for external parasites varies, depending upon the parasite involved, but a number of good dips and powders are available.

Fleas may be eliminated by dusting the coat thoroughly with flea powder at frequent intervals during the summer months when fleas are a problem.

Flea collars are very effective in keeping a dog free of fleas. However, some animals are allergic to the chemicals in the collars, so caution must be observed when the collar is used and the skin of the neck area must be checked frequently and the collar removed if the skin becomes irritated. Care must also be taken that the collar is not fastened too tightly, and any excess at the end must be cut off to prevent the dog from chewing it. The collar should be removed if it becomes wet (or even damp) and should always be removed before the dog is bathed and not replaced around the dog's neck again until the coat is completely dry. For a dog which reacts to the flea collar, a medallion to be hung from the regular collar is available. This will eliminate direct skin contact and thus any allergic reaction will be avoided. The medallion should, of course, be removed when the dog is bathed.

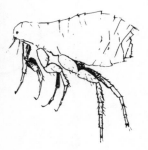

Dog flea (much enlarged).

American dog tick, female (much enlarged).

American dog tick, male (much enlarged).

Female dog tick engorged.

Lice may be eradicated by applying dips formulated especially for this purpose to the dog's coat. A fine-toothed comb should then be used to remove dead lice and eggs, which are firmly attached to the coat.

Mites live deep in the ear canal, producing irritation to the lining of the ear and causing a brownish-black, dry type discharge. Plain mineral oil or ear ointment should be swabbed on the inner surface of the ear twice a week until mites are eliminated.

Ticks may carry Rocky Mountain spotted fever, so, to avoid possible infection, they should be removed from the dog only with tweezers and should be destroyed by burning (or by dropping them into insecticide). Heavy infestation can be controlled by sponging the coat daily with a solution containing a special tick dip.

Among other preparations available for controlling parasites on the dog's body are some that can be given internally. Since dosage must be carefully controlled, these preparations should not be used without consulting a veterinarian.

Internal Parasites

Internal parasites, with the exception of the tapeworm, may be transmitted from a mother dog to the puppies. Infestation may also result from contact with infected bedding or through access to a yard where an infected dog relieves himself. The types that may infest dogs are roundworms, whipworms, tapeworms, hook-worms, and heartworms. All cause similar symptoms: a generally unthrifty appearance, stary coat, dull eyes, weakness and emaciation despite a ravenous appetite, coughing, vomiting, diarrhea, and sometimes bloody stools. Not all symptoms are present in every case, of course.

A heavy infestation with any type of worm is a serious matter and treatment must be started early and continued

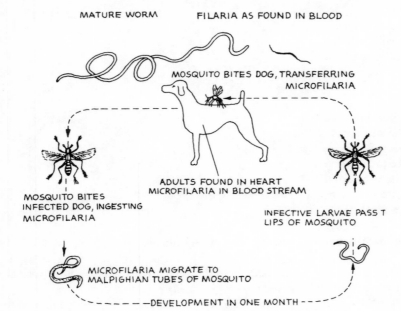

MATURE WORM   FILARIA AS FOUND IN BLOOD

MOSQUITO BITES DOG, TRANSFERRING
MICROFILARIA

LIFE CYCLE OF
THE HEARTWORM

ADULTS FOUND IN HEART
MICROFILARIA IN BLOOD STREAM

MOSQUITO BITES
INFECTED DOG, INGESTING
MICROFILARIA

INFECTIVE LARVAE PASS T
LIPS OF MOSQUITO

MICROFILARIA MIGRATE TO
MALPIGHIAN TUBES OF MOSQUITO

------ DEVELOPMENT IN ONE MONTH ----

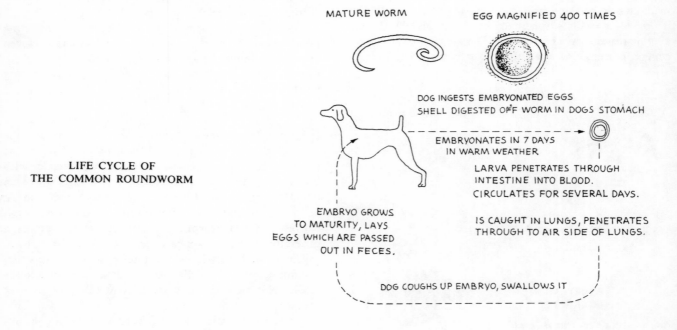

MATURE WORM   EGG MAGNIFIED 400 TIMES

DOG INGESTS EMBRYONATED EGGS
SHELL DIGESTED OFF WORM IN DOGS STOMACH

EMBRYONATES IN 7 DAYS
IN WARM WEATHER

LIFE CYCLE OF
THE COMMON ROUNDWORM

LARVA PENETRATES THROUGH
INTESTINE INTO BLOOD.
CIRCULATES FOR SEVERAL DAYS.

IS CAUGHT IN LUNGS, PENETRATES
THROUGH TO AIR SIDE OF LUNGS.

EMBRYO GROWS
TO MATURITY, LAYS
EGGS WHICH ARE PASSED
OUT IN FECES.

DOG COUGHS UP EMBRYO, SWALLOWS IT

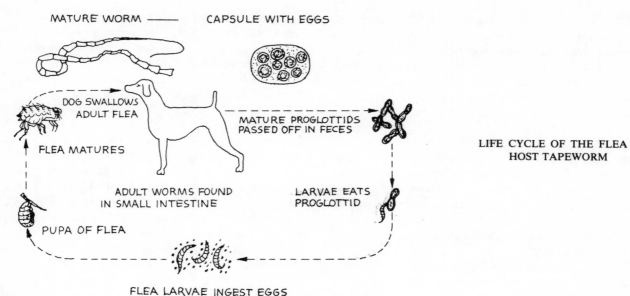

MATURE WORM ——— CAPSULE WITH EGGS

DOG SWALLOWS ADULT FLEA

MATURE PROGLOTTIDS PASSED OFF IN FECES

LIFE CYCLE OF THE FLEA HOST TAPEWORM

FLEA MATURES

ADULT WORMS FOUND IN SMALL INTESTINE

LARVAE EATS PROGLOTTID

PUPA OF FLEA

FLEA LARVAE INGEST EGGS

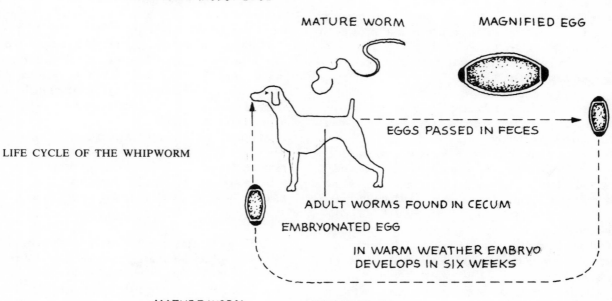

MATURE WORM   MAGNIFIED EGG

EGGS PASSED IN FECES

LIFE CYCLE OF THE WHIPWORM

ADULT WORMS FOUND IN CECUM

EMBRYONATED EGG

IN WARM WEATHER EMBRYO DEVELOPS IN SIX WEEKS

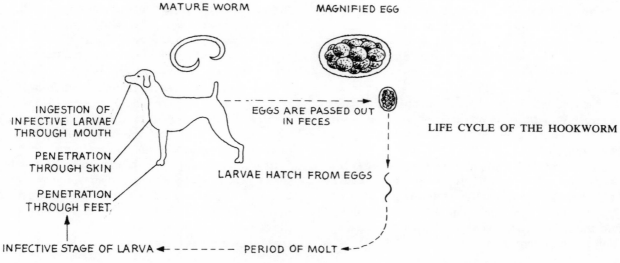

MATURE WORM   MAGNIFIED EGG

INGESTION OF INFECTIVE LARVAE THROUGH MOUTH

EGGS ARE PASSED OUT IN FECES

LIFE CYCLE OF THE HOOKWORM

PENETRATION THROUGH SKIN

PENETRATION THROUGH FEET.

LARVAE HATCH FROM EGGS

INFECTIVE STAGE OF LARVA ◄— — — — PERIOD OF MOLT ◄— —

until the dog is free of the parasite or the dog's health will suffer seriously. Death may even result.

Promiscuous dosing for worms is dangerous and different types of worms require different treatment. So if you suspect your dog has worms, ask your veterinarian to make a microscopic examination of the feces, and to prescribe appropriate treatment if evidence of worm infestation is found.

Heartworms, once thought to be a problem confined to the Southern part of the United States, today represent a life-threatening danger to dogs in all parts of the country. Heartworm larvae are transmitted from dog to dog through the bite of the mosquito. Once they have entered the bloodstream, heartworms mature in the heart, where they interfere with heart action, causing chronic coughing and labored breathing.

The tiny heartworm larvae (called microfilariae) can be detected only through microscopic examination of the dog's blood. Effective preventive medication is available but can be given only if the microscopic examination shows that no microfilariae are present. While medication is also available for treating infested dogs, the degree of success to be expected depends upon the amount of damage already sustained.

Because of the radical nature of the treatment required once infestation occurs, prevention is by far the preferred approach. A veterinarian should be consulted and his advice followed implicitly.

Hookworms are found in puppies as well as adult dogs. When excreted in the feces, the mature worm looks like a thread and is about three-quarters of an inch in length. Eradication is a serious problem in areas where the soil is infested with the worms, for the dog may then become reinfested after treatment. Consequently, medication usually must be repeated at intervals, and the premises—including the grounds where the dog exercises—must be treated and must be kept well drained. You may wish to consult your veterinarian regarding the vaccine for the prevention of hookworms in dogs which was licensed recently by the United States Department of Agriculture.

Roundworms are the most common of all the worms that may infest the dog, for most puppies are born with them or become infested with them shortly after birth. Roundworms vary in length from two to eight inches and can be detected readily through microscopic examination of the feces. At maturity, upon excretion, the roundworm will spiral into a circle, but after it dies it resembles a cut rubber band.

If you suspect that a puppy may have roundworms, check its gums and tongue. If the puppy is heavily infested, the worms will cause anemia and the gums and the tongue will be a very pale pink color. If the puppy is anemic, the veterinarian probably will prescribe a tonic in addition to the proper worm medicine.

Tapeworms require an intermediate host, usually the flea or the louse, but they sometimes are found in raw fish, so a dog can become infested by swallowing a flea or a louse, or by eating infested fish.

A complete tapeworm can be two to three feet long. The head and neck of the tapeworm are small and threadlike, while the body is made up of segments like links of a sausage, which are about half an inch long and flat. Segments of the body separate from the worm and will be found in the feces or will hang from the coat around the anus and when dry will resemble dark grains of rice.

The head of the tapeworm is imbedded in the lining of the intestine where the worm feeds on the blood of the dog. The difficulty in eradicating the tapeworm lies in the fact that most medicines have a laxative action which is too severe and which pulls the body from the head so the body is eliminated with the feces, but the implanted head remains to start growing a new body. An effective medication is a tablet which does not dissolve until it reaches the intestine where it anesthetizes the worm to loosen the head before expulsion.

Whipworms are more common in the eastern states than in states along the West Coast, but whipworms may infest dogs in any section of the United States. Whipworms vary in length from two to four inches and are tapered in shape so they resemble a buggy whip—which accounts for the name.

At maturity, the whipworm migrates into the caecum, where it is difficult to reach with medication. A fecal examination will show whether whipworms are present, so after treatment, it is best to have several examinations made in order to be sure the dog is free of them.

Skin Problems

Skin problems usually cause persistent itching. However, **follicular mange** does not usually do so but is evidenced by moth-eaten-looking patches, especially about the head and along the back. **Sarcoptic mange** produces severe itching and is evidenced by patchy, crusty areas on body, legs, and abdomen. Any evidence suggesting either should be called to the attention of a veterinarian. Both require extensive treatment and both may be contracted by humans.

Allergies are not readily distinguished from other skin troubles except through laboratory tests. However, dog owners should be alert to the fact that various coat dressings and shampoos, or simply bathing the dog too often, may produce allergic skin reactions.

Eczema is characterized by extreme itching, redness of the skin and exudation of serous matter. It may result from a variety of causes, and the exact cause in a particular case may be difficult to determine. Relief may be secured by dusting the dog twice a week with a soothing powder containing a fungicide and an insecticide.

Other Health Problems

Clogged anal glands cause intense discomfort, which the dog may attempt to relieve by scooting himself along the floor on his haunches. These glands, located on either side of the anus, secrete a substance that enables the dog to expel the contents of the rectum. If they become clogged, they may give the dog an unpleasant odor and when neglected, serious infection may result. Contents of the glands can be easily expelled into a wad of cotton, which should be held under the tail with the left hand. Then, using the right hand, pressure should be exerted with the thumb on one side of the anus, the forefinger on the other. The normal secretion is brownish in color, with an unpleasant odor. The presence of blood or pus indicates infection and should be called to the attention of the veterinarian.

Eye problems of a minor nature—redness or occasional discharge—may be treated with a few drops of boric acid solution (2%) or salt solution (1 teaspoonful table salt to 1 pint sterile water). Cuts on the eyeball, bruises close to the eyes, or persistent discharge should be treated only by a veterinarian.

Heat exhaustion is a serious (and often fatal) problem caused by exposure to extreme heat. Usually it occurs when a thoughtless owner leaves the dog in a closed vehicle without proper shade and ventilation. Even on a day when outside temperatures do not seem excessively high, heat builds up rapidly to an extremely high temperature in a closed vehicle parked in direct sunlight or even in partial shade. Many dogs and young children die each year from being left in an inadequately ventilated vehicle. To prevent such a tragedy, an owner or parent should never leave a dog or child unattended in a vehicle even for a short time.

During hot weather, whenever a dog is taken for a ride in an air-conditioned automobile, the cool air should be reduced gradually when nearing the destination, for the sudden shock of going from cool air to extremely hot temperatures can also result in shock and heat exhaustion.

Symptoms of heat exhaustion include rapid and difficult breathing and near or complete collapse. After removing the victim from the vehicle, first aid treatment consists of sponging cool water over the body to reduce temperature as quickly as possible. Immediate medical treatment is essential in severe cases of heat exhaustion.

Care of the Ailing or Injured Dog

A dog that is seriously ill, requiring surgical treatment, transfusions, or intravenous feeding, must be hospitalized. One requiring less complicated treatment is better cared for at home, but it is essential that the dog be kept in a quiet environment. Preferably his bed should be in a room apart from family activity, yet close at hand, so his condition can be checked frequently. Clean bedding and adequate warmth are essential, as are a constant supply of fresh, cool water, and foods to tempt the appetite.

Special equipment is not ordinarily needed, but the following items will be useful in caring for a sick dog, as well as in giving first aid for injuries:

petroleum jelly	tincture of metaphen
rubbing alcohol	cotton, gauze, and
mineral oil	adhesive tape
rectal thermometer	burn ointment
hydrogen peroxide	tweezers
boric acid solution (2%)	

If special medication is prescribed, it may be administered in any one of several ways. A pill or small capsule may be concealed in a small piece of meat, which the dog will usually swallow with no problem. A large capsule may be given by holding the dog's mouth open, inserting the capsule as far as possible down the throat, then holding the mouth closed until the dog swallows. Liquid medicine should be measured into a small bottle or test tube. Then, if the corner of the dog's lip is pulled out while the head is tilted upward, the liquid can be poured between the lips and teeth, a small amount at a time. If he refuses to swallow, keeping the dog's head tilted and stroking his throat will usually induce swallowing.

Liquid medication may also be given by use of a hypodermic syringe without a needle. The syringe is slipped into the side of the mouth and over the rise at the back of the tongue, and the medicine is "injected" slowly down the throat. This is especially good for medicine with a bad taste, for the medicine does not touch the taste buds in the front part of the tongue. It also eliminates spills and guarantees that all the medicine goes in.

Foods offered the sick dog should be nutritious and easily digested. Meals should be smaller than usual and offered at more frequent intervals. If the dog is reluctant to eat, offer food he particularly likes. Warm it slightly to increase aroma and make it more tempting.

Ch. Zamorane, C.D.X. BOS at the 1953 BSCA National Specialty. (Ubro of the Country House x Xivlette.) Owners, Robert and Barbara Krohn.

Ch. Fleur Ebon de Beaute Noir, C.D. (Francois du Chemin Des Dames x Rose du Groenendael.) Owners, Rush and Shirley Brown.

Ch. Liza del Pirata Nero, C.D. BOS at the 1956 BSCA National Specialty. (Zordoff x Sjla del Pirata Nero.) Owners, Marge and Ed Turnquist.

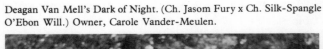

Deagan Van Mell's Dark of Night. (Ch. Jasom Fury x Ch. Silk-Spangle O'Ebon Will.) Owner, Carole Vander-Meulen.

Manners for the Family Dog

Although each dog has personality quirks and idiosyncrasies that set him apart as an individual, dogs in general have two characteristics that can be utilized to advantage in training. The first is the dog's strong desire to please, which has been built up through centuries of association with man. The second lies in the innate quality of the dog's mentality. It has been proved conclusively that while dogs have reasoning power, their learning ability is based on a direct association of cause and effect, so that they willingly repeat acts that bring pleasant results and discontinue acts that bring unpleasant results. Hence, to take fullest advantage of a dog's abilities, the trainer must make sure the dog understands a command, and then reward him when he obeys and correct him when he does wrong.

Commands should be as short as possible and should be repeated in the same way, day after day. Saying "Heel," one day, and "Come here and heel," the next will confuse the dog. *Heel, sit, stand, stay, down,* and *come* are standard terminology, and are preferable for a dog that may later be given advanced training.

Tone of voice is important, too. For instance, a coaxing tone helps cajole a young puppy into trying something new. Once an exercise is mastered, commands given in a firm, matter-of-fact voice give the dog confidence in his own ability. Praise, expressed in an exuberant tone, will tell the dog quite clearly that he has earned his master's approval. On the other hand, a firm "No" indicates with equal clarity that he has done wrong.

Rewards for good performance may consist simply of praising lavishly and petting the dog, although many professional trainers use bits of food as rewards. Tidbits are effective only if the dog is hungry, of course. And if you smoke, you must be sure to wash your hands before each training session, for the odor of nicotine is repulsive to dogs. On the hands of a heavy smoker, the odor of nicotine may be so strong that the dog is unable to smell the tidbit.

Correction for wrong-doing should be limited to repeating "No" in a scolding tone of voice or to confining the dog to his bed. Spanking or striking the dog is taboo—particularly using sticks, which might cause injury, but the hand should never be used either. For field training as well as some obedience work, the hand is used to signal the dog. Dogs that have been punished by slapping have a tendency to cringe whenever they see a hand raised and consequently do not respond promptly when the owner's intent is not to punish but to signal.

Some trainers recommend correcting the dog by whacking him with a rolled-up newspaper. The idea is that the newspaper will not injure the dog but that the resulting noise will condition the dog to avoid repeating the act that seemingly caused the noise. Many authorities object to this type of correction, for it may result in the dog's becoming "noise-shy"—a decided disadvantage with show dogs which must maintain poise in adverse, often noisy, situations. "Noise-shyness" is also an unfortunate reaction in field dogs, since it may lead to gun-shyness.

To be effective, correction must be administered immediately, so that in the dog's mind there is a direct connection between his act and the correction. You can make voice corrections under almost any circumstances, but you must never call the dog to you and then correct him, or he will associate the correction with the fact that he has come and will become reluctant to respond. If the dog is at a distance and doing something he shouldn't, go to him and scold him while he is still involved in wrong-doing. If this is impossible, ignore the offense until he repeats it and you can correct him properly.

Especially while a dog is young, he should be watched closely and stopped before he gets into mischief. All dogs need to do a certain amount of chewing, so to prevent your puppy's chewing something you value, provide him with his own balls and toys. Never allow him to chew castoff slippers and then expect him to differentiate between cast-off items and those you value. Nylon stockings, wooden articles, and various other items may cause intestinal obstructions if the dog chews and swallows them, and death may result. So it is essential that the dog be permitted to chew only on bones or toys that he cannot chew up or swallow.

Serious training for obedience should not be started until a dog is a year old. But basic training in house manners should begin the day the puppy enters his new home. A puppy should never be given the run of the house but should be confined to a box or small pen except for play periods when you can devote full attention to him. The first thing to teach the dog is his name, so that whenever he hears it, he will immediately come to attention. Whenever you are near his box, talk to him, using his name repeatedly. During play periods, talk to him, pet him, and handle him, for he must be conditioned so he will not object to being handled by a veterinarian, show judge, or family friend. As the dog investigates his surroundings, watch him carefully and if he tries something he shouldn't, reprimand him with a scolding "No!" If he repeats the offense, scold him and confine him to his box, then praise him. Discipline must be prompt, consistent, and always followed with praise. Never tease the dog, and never allow others to do so. Kindness and understanding are essential to a pleasant, mutually rewarding relationship.

When the puppy is two to three months old, secure a flat, narrow leather collar and have him start wearing it

Left, Ch. Fleur Ebon IV. (Ch. Tazir del Pirata Nero x Ch. Fleur Ebon III.) Owners, Rush and Shirley Brown.

Ch. Roll-In Fame. Owners, Myron and Freda Rowland. (From a postcard, "Purebred Belgian Sheepdog.")

Ch. Midnight Satin O'Deartrail, C.D. (Ch. Guilded Knight O'Ebon Will, C.D. x Ch. Evening Lace O'Ebon Will.) Owner, Shirley Howard.

Ch. Chandler's Pandora. Owners, Sam and Freda Chandler.

Left, Ch. Quilhot's Lupo Nero, BOB, 1961 BSCA National Specialty. (Ch. Zulvo, C.D. x Jean Suzette, C.D.) Owners, Myron and Freda Rowland.

(never use a harness, which will encourage tugging and pulling). After a week or so, attach a light leather leash to the collar during play sessions and let the puppy walk around, dragging the leash behind him. Then start holding the end of the leash and coaxing the puppy to come to you. He will then be fully accustomed to collar and leash when you start taking him outside while he is being housebroken.

Housebreaking can be accomplished in a matter of approximately two weeks provided you wait until the dog is mature enough to have some control over bodily functions. This is usually at about four months. Until that time, the puppy should spend most of his day confined to his penned area, with the floor covered with several thicknesses of newspapers so that he may relieve himself when necessary without damage to floors.

Either of two methods works well in housebreaking— the choice depending upon where you live. If you live in a house with a readily accessible yard, you will probably want to train the puppy from the beginning to go outdoors. If you live in an apartment without easy access to a yard, you may decide to train him first to relieve himself on newspapers and then when he has learned control, to teach the puppy to go outdoors.

If you decide to train the puppy by taking him outdoors, arrange some means of confining him indoors where you can watch him closely—in a small penned area, or tied to a short leash (five or six feet). Dogs are naturally clean animals, reluctant to soil their quarters, and confining the puppy to a limited area will encourage him to avoid making a mess.

A young puppy must be taken out often, so watch your puppy closely and if he indicates he is about to relieve himself, take him out at once. If he has an accident, scold him and take him out so he will associate the act of going outside with the need to relieve himself. Always take the puppy out within an hour after meals—preferably to the same place each time—and make sure he relieves himself before you return him to the house. Restrict his water for two hours before bedtime and take him out just before you retire for the night. Then, as soon as you wake in the morning, take him out again.

For paper training, set aside a particular room and cover a large area of the floor with several thicknesses of newspapers. Confine the dog on a short leash and each time he relieves himself, remove the soiled papers and replace them with clean ones.

As his control increases, gradually decrease the paper area, leaving part of the floor bare. If he uses the bare floor, scold him mildly and put him on the papers, letting him know that there is where he is to relieve himself. As he comes to understand the idea, increase the bare area until papers cover only space equal to approximately two full newspaper sheets. Keep him using the papers, but begin

Chain-link collar. The collar should be removed whenever the dog is not under your immediate supervision, for many dogs have met death by strangulation when a collar was left on and became entangled in some object.

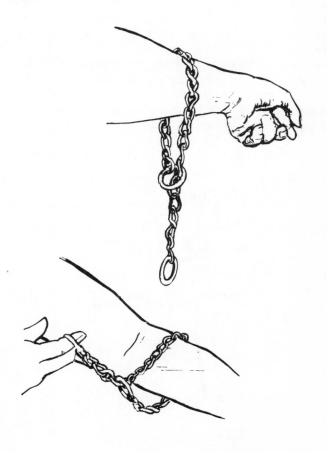

41

taking him out on a leash at the times of day that he habitually relieves himself. Watch him closely when he is indoors and at the first sign that he needs to go, take him outdoors. Restrict his water for two hours before bedtime, but if necessary, permit him to use the papers before you retire for the night.

Using either method, the puppy will be housebroken in an amazingly short time. Once he has learned control he will need to relieve himself only four or five times a day.

Informal obedience training, started at the age of about six to eight months, will provide a good background for any advanced training you may decide to give your dog later. The collar most effective for training is the metal chain-link variety. The correct size for your dog will be about one inch longer than the measurement around the largest part of his head. The chain must be slipped through one of the rings so the collar forms a loop. The collar should be put on with the loose ring at the right of the dog's neck, the chain attached to it coming over the neck and through the holding ring, rather than under the neck. Since the dog is to be at your left for most of the training, this makes the collar most effective.

The leash should be attached to the loose ring, and should be either webbing or leather, six feet long and a half inch to a full inch wide. When you want your dog's attention, or wish to correct him, give a light, quick pull on the leash, which will momentarily tighten the collar about the neck. Release the pressure instantly, and the correction will have been made. If the puppy is already accustomed to a leather collar, he will adjust easily to the training collar. But before you start training sessions, practice walking with the dog until he responds readily when you increase tension on the leash.

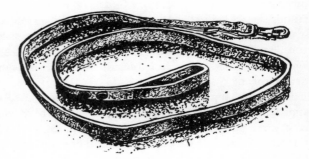

Six-foot leash.

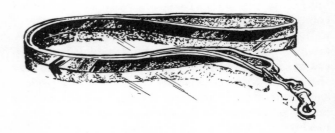

Three-foot leash.

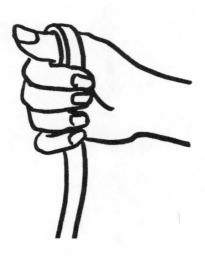

Correct way to hold leash.

Set aside a period of fifteen minutes, once or twice a day, for regular training sessions, and train in a place where there will be no distractions. Teach only one exercise at a time, making sure the dog has mastered it before going on to another. It will probably take at least a week for the dog to master each exercise. As training progresses, start each session by reviewing exercises the dog has already learned, then go on to the new exercise for a period of concerted practice. When discipline is required, make the correction immediately, and always praise the dog after corrections as well as when he obeys promptly. During each session stick strictly to business. Afterwards, take time to play with the dog.

The first exercise to teach is heeling. Have the dog at

your left and hold the leash as shown in the illustration on the preceding page. Start walking, and just as you put your foot forward for the first step, say your dog's name to get his attention, followed by the command "Heel!" Simultaneously, pull on the leash lightly. As you walk, try to keep the dog at your left side, with his head alongside your left leg. Pull on the leash as necessary to urge him forward or back, to right or left, but keep him in position. Each time you pull on the leash, say "Heel!" and praise the dog lavishly. When the dog heels properly in a straight line, start making circles, turning corners, etc.

Once the dog has learned to heel well, start teaching the "sit." Each time you stop while heeling, command "Sit!" The dog will be at your left, so use your left hand to press on his rear and guide him to a sitting position, while you use the leash in your right hand to keep his head up. Hold him in position for a few moments while you praise him, then give the command to heel. Walk a few steps, stop, and repeat the procedure. Before long he will automatically sit whenever you stop. You can then teach the dog to "sit" from any position.

When the dog will sit on command without correction, he is ready to learn to stay until you release him. Simply sit him, command "Stay!" and hold him in position for perhaps half a minute, repeating "Stay," if he attempts to stand. You can release him by saying "O.K." Gradually increase the time until he will stay on command for three or four minutes.

The "stand-stay" should also be taught when the dog is on leash. While you are heeling, stop and give the command "Stand!" Keep the dog from sitting by quickly placing your left arm under him, immediately in front of his right leg. If he continues to try to sit, don't scold him but start up again with the heel command, walk a few steps, and stop again, repeating the stand command and preventing the dog from sitting. Once the dog has mastered the stand, teach him to stay by holding him in position and repeating the word "Stay!"

The "down stay" will prove beneficial in many situations, but especially if you wish to take your dog in the car without confining him to a crate. To teach the "down," have the dog sitting at your side with collar and leash on. If he is a large dog, step forward with the leash in your hand and turn so you face him. Let the leash touch the floor, then step over it with your right foot so it is under the instep of your shoe. Grasping the leash low down with both hands, slowly pull up, saying "Down!" Hold the leash taut until the dog goes down. Once he responds well, teach the dog to stay in the down position (the down-stay), using the same method as for the sit- and stand-stays.

To teach small dogs the "down," another method may be used. Have the dog sit at your side, then kneel beside him. Reach across his back with your left arm, and take hold of his left front leg close to the body. At the same time, with your right hand take hold of his right front leg close to his body. As you command "Down!" gently lift the legs and place the dog in the down position. Release your hold on his legs and slide your left hand onto his back, repeating, "Down, stay," while keeping him in position.

The "come" is taught when the dog is on leash and heeling. Simply walk along, then suddenly take a step backward, saying "Come!" Pull the leash as you give the command and the dog will turn and follow you. Continue walking backward, repeatedly saying "Come," and tightening the leash if necessary.

Once the dog has mastered the exercises while on leash, try taking the leash off and going through the same routine, beginning with the heeling exercise. If the dog doesn't respond promptly, he needs review with the leash on. But patience and persistence will be rewarded, for you will have a dog you can trust to respond promptly under all conditions.

Even after they are well trained, dogs sometimes develop bad habits that are hard to break. Jumping on people is a common habit, and all members of the family must assist if it is to be broken. If the dog is a large or medium breed, take a step forward and raise your knee just as he starts to jump on you. As your knee strikes the dog's chest, command "Down!" in a scolding voice. When a small dog jumps on you, take both front paws in your hands, and, while talking in a pleasant tone of voice, step on the dog's back feet just hard enough to hurt them slightly. With either method the dog is taken by surprise and doesn't associate the discomfort with the person causing it.

Occasionally a dog may be too chummy with guests who don't care for dogs. If the dog has had obedience training, simply command "Come!" When he responds, have him sit beside you.

Persistent efforts may be needed to subdue a dog that barks without provocation. To correct the habit, you must be close to the dog when he starts barking. Encircle his muzzle with both hands, hold his mouth shut, and command "Quiet!" in a firm voice. He should soon learn to respond so you can control him simply by giving the command.

Sniffing other dogs is an annoying habit. If the dog is off leash and sniffs other dogs, ignoring your commands to come, he needs to review the lessons on basic behavior. When the dog is on leash, scold him, then pull on the leash, command "Heel," and walk away from the other dog.

A well-trained dog will be no problem if you decide to take him with you when you travel. No matter how well he responds, however, he should never be permitted off leash when you walk him in a strange area. Distractions will be more tempting, and there will be more chance of his being attacked by other dogs. So whenever the dog travels with you, take his collar and leash along—and use them.

I CAN TEACH HIM

Above, Ch. Laralee's Personality, C.D.X., A.D., Sch-H I. (Am. and Eng. Ch. Laralee's Traveler x Ch. Vicci's Tamarin.) Owner, Pat Crabtree.

Left, Val Valle Chieho's My Own Belle and Val Valle Micco. Owner, Cathy Ewing.

Below, Sheba III de Beaute Noir, U.D., and Ch. Dulci Candide, C.D., pulling a cart for fun. Owner, Rudy Robinson.

44

Show Competition

Centuries ago, it was common practice to hold agricultural fairs in conjunction with spring and fall religious festivals, and to these gatherings, cattle, dogs, and other livestock were brought for exchange. As time went on, it became customary to provide entertainment, too. Dogs often participated in such sporting events as bull baiting, bear baiting, and ratting. Then the dog that exhibited the greatest skill in the arena was also the one that brought the highest price when time came for barter or sale. Today, these fairs seem a far cry from our highly organized bench shows and field trials. But they were the forerunners of modern dog shows and played an important role in shaping the development of purebred dogs.

The first organized dog show was held at Newcastle, England, in 1859. Later that same year, a show was held at Birmingham. At both shows dogs were divided into four classes and only Pointers and Setters were entered. In 1860, the first dog show in Germany was held at Apoldo, where nearly one hundred dogs were exhibited and entries were divided into six groups. Interest expanded rapidly, and by the time the Paris Exhibition was held in 1878, the dog show was a fixture of international importance.

In the United States, the first organized bench show was held in 1874 in conjunction with the meeting of the Illinois State Sportsmen's Association in Chicago, and all entries were dogs of sporting breeds. Although the show was a rather casual affair, interest spread quickly. Before the end of the year, shows were held in Oswego, New York, Mineola, Long Island, and Memphis, Tennessee. And the latter combined a bench show with the first organized field trial ever held in the United States. In January 1875, an all-breed show (the first in the United States) was held at Detroit, Michigan. From then on, interest increased rapidly, though rules were not always uniform, for there was no organization through which to coordinate activities until September 1884 when The American Kennel Club was founded. Now the largest dog registering organization in the world, the AKC is an association of several hundred member clubs—all breed, specialty, field trial, and obedience groups—each represented by a delegate to the AKC.

The several thousand shows and trials held annually in the United States do much to stimulate interest in breeding to produce better looking, sounder, purebred dogs. For breeders, shows provide a means of measuring the merits of their work as compared with accomplishments of other breeders. For hundreds of thousands of dog fanciers, they provide an absorbing hobby.

Benching area at Westminster Kennel Club Show.

Junior Showmanship Competition at Westminster Kennel Club Show.

Judging for Best in Show at Westminster Kennel Club Show.

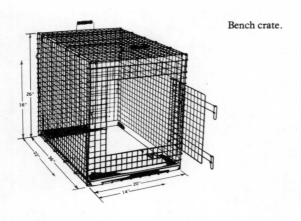

Bench crate.

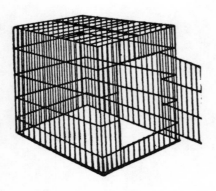

Collapsible cage.

Wagon crate.

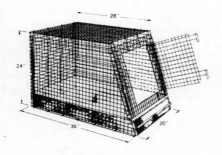

Bench Shows

At bench (or conformation) shows, dogs are rated comparatively on their physical qualities (or conformation) in accordance with breed Standards which have been approved by The American Kennel Club. Characteristics such as size, coat, color, placement of eye or ear, general soundness, etc., are the basis of selecting the best dog in a class. Only purebred dogs are eligible to compete and if the show is one where points toward a championship are to be awarded, a dog must be at least six months old.

Bench shows are of various types. An all-breed show has classes for all of the breeds recognized by The American Kennel Club as well as a Miscellaneous Class for breeds not recognized, such as the Australian Cattle Dog, the Ibizan Hound, the Spinoni Italiani, etc. A sanctioned match is an informal meeting where dogs compete but not for championship points. A specialty show is confined to a single breed. Other shows may restrict entries to champions of record, to American-bred dogs, etc. Competition for Junior Showmanship or for Best Brace, Best Team, or Best Local Dog may be included. Also, obedience competition is held in conjunction with many bench shows.

The term "bench show" is somewhat confusing in that shows of this type may be either "benched" or "unbenched." At the former, each dog is assigned an individual numbered stall where he must remain throughout the show except for times when he is being judged, groomed, or exercised. At unbenched shows, no stalls are provided and dogs are kept in their owners' cars or in crates when not being judged.

A show where a dog is judged for conformation actually constitutes an elimination contest. To begin with, the dogs of a single breed compete with others of their breed in one of the regular classes: Puppy, Novice, Bred by Exhibitor, American-Bred, or Open, and finally, Winners, where the top dogs of the preceding five classes meet. The next step is the judging for Best of Breed (or Best of Variety of Breed). Here the Winners Dog and Winners Bitch (or the dog named Winners if only one prize is awarded) compete with any champions that are entered, together with any undefeated dogs that have competed in additional non-regular classes. The dog named Best of Breed (or Best of Variety of Breed) then goes on to compete with the other Best of Breed winners in his Group. The dogs that win in Group competition then compete for the final and highest honor, Best in Show.

When the Winners Class is divided by sex, championship points are awarded the Winners Dog and Winners Bitch. If the Winners Class is not divided by sex, championship points are awarded the dog or bitch named Winners. The number of points awarded varies, depending upon such factors as the number of dogs competing, the Schedule of Points established by the Board of Directors of the AKC, and whether the dog goes on to win Best of Breed, the Group, and Best in Show.

In order to become a champion, a dog must win fifteen points, including points from at least two major wins— that is, at least two shows where three or more points are awarded. The major wins must be under two different judges, and one or more of the remaining points must be won under a third judge. The most points ever awarded at a show is five and the least is one, so, in order to become a champion, a dog must be exhibited and win in at least three shows, and usually he is shown many times before he wins his championship.

Pure Bred Dogs—American Kennel Gazette and other dog magazines contain lists of forthcoming shows, together with names and addresses of sponsoring organizations to which you may write for entry forms and information relative to fees, closing dates, etc. Before entering your dog in a show for the first time, you should familiarize yourself with the regulations and rules governing competition. You may secure such information from The American Kennel Club or from a local dog club specializing in your breed. It is essential that you also familiarize yourself with the AKC approved Standard for your breed so you will be fully aware of characteristics worthy of merit as well as those considered faulty, or possibly even serious enough to disqualify the dog from competition. For instance, monorchidism (failure of one testicle to descend) and cryptorchidism (failure of both testicles to descend) are disqualifying faults in all breeds.

If possible, you should first attend a show as a spectator and observe judging procedures from ringside. It will also be helpful to join a local breed club and to participate in sanctioned matches before entering an all-breed show.

The dog should be equipped with a narrow leather show lead and a show collar—never an ornamented or spiked collar. For benched shows, either a bench crate, or a metal-link bench chain to fasten the dog to the bench, will be needed. For unbenched shows, the dog's crate should be taken along so that he may be confined in comfort when he is not appearing in the ring. A dog should never be left in a car with all the windows closed. In hot weather the temperature will become unbearable in a very short time. Heat exhaustion may result from even a short period of confinement, and death may ensue.

Food and water dishes will be needed, as well as a supply of the food and water to which the dog is accustomed. Brushes and combs are also necessary, so that you may give the dog's coat a final grooming after you arrive at the show.

Familiarize yourself with the schedule of classes ahead of time, for the dog must be fed and exercised and permitted to relieve himself, and any last-minute grooming completed before his class is called. Both you

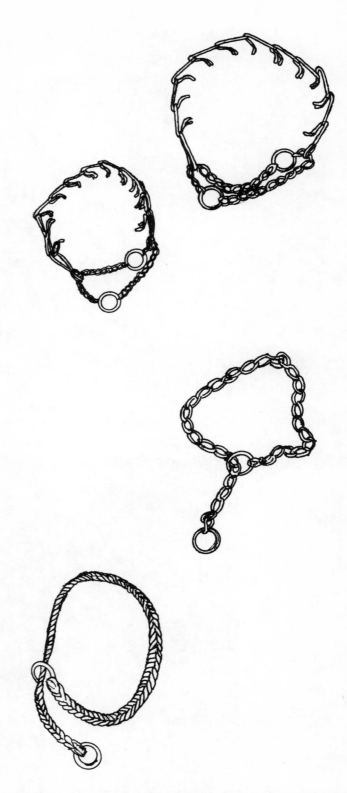

Collars. At the top are two "pinch" or "spiked" collars that are not permitted in AKC shows. Below are two permissible "choke" collars. The one on the right is of steel chain and the one on the left is of braided nylon. While the choke collars are permitted in conformation shows, they are used more often in obedience competition.

Left to right: Bill Vestal, Judge Anton Korbel, Clara Vestal, John Ross. Dogs, left to right: Rita Vixen de Belgique; Thor, C.D.X.; Hadji de Flanders, U.D.T.; and Bo-Negra del Rio Carmello. 1949 Palm Springs Kennel Club Show.

Joe Mainville and Mahoja guarding the campsite. Owners, Frank and Artice Mainville. Photo by Frank Mainville.

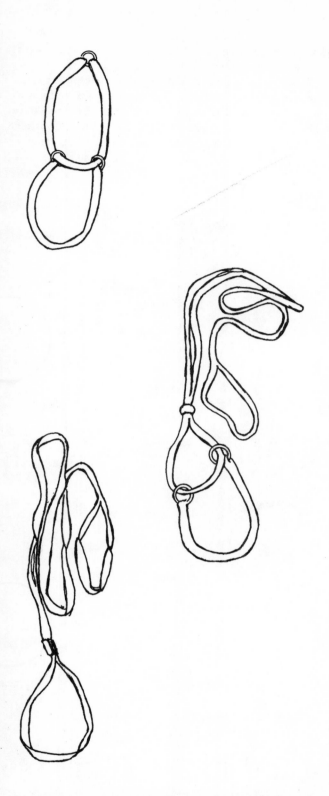

Top, "English" or "Martingale" collar to which lead would be attached. Center, "English" or "Martingale" collar and lead. In using either of these, the dog's head would be inserted through the lower loop. Bottom, nylon slip lead. Collars and leads of these three types are preferred for conformation showing because they give better control for stacking a dog than does the "choke" collar.

and the dog should be ready to enter the ring unhurriedly. A good deal of skill in conditioning, training, and handling is required if a dog is to be presented properly. And it is essential that the handler himself be composed, for a jittery handler will transmit his nervousness to his dog.

Once the class is assembled in the ring, the judge will ask that the dogs be paraded in line, moving counter-clockwise in a circle. If you have trained your dog well, you will have no difficulty controlling him in the ring, where he must change pace quickly and gracefully and walk and trot elegantly and proudly with head erect. The show dog must also stand quietly for inspection, posing like a statue for several minutes while the judge observes his structure in detail, examines teeth, feet, coat, etc. When the judge calls your dog forward for individual inspection, do not attempt to converse, but answer any questions he may ask.

As the judge examines the class, he measures each dog against the ideal described in the Standard, then measures the dogs against each other in a comparative sense and selects for first place the dog that comes closest to conforming to the Standard for its breed. If your dog isn't among the winners, don't grumble. If he places first, don't brag loudly. For a bad loser is disgusting, but a poor winner is insufferable.

Obedience Competition

For hundreds of years, dogs have been used in England and Germany in connection with police and guard work, and their working potential has been evaluated through tests devised to show agility, strength, and courage. Organized training has also been popular with English and German breeders for many years, although it was practiced primarily for the purpose of training large breeds in aggressive tactics.

There was little interest in obedience training in the United States until 1933 when Mrs. Whitehouse Walker returned from England and enthusiastically introduced the sport. Two years later, Mrs. Walker persuaded The American Kennel Club to approve organized obedience activities and to assume jurisdiction over obedience rules. Since then, interest has increased at a phenomenal rate, for obedience competition is not only a sport the average spectator can follow readily, but also a sport for which the average owner can train his own dog easily. Obedience competition is suitable for all breeds. Furthermore, there is no limit to the number of dogs that may win in competition, for each dog is scored individually on the basis of a point rating system.

The dog is judged on his response to certain commands, and if he gains a high enough score in three successive trials under different judges, he wins an obedience title. Titles awarded are "C.D."—Companion Dog; "C.D.X." —Companion Dog Excellent; and "U.D."—Utility Dog. A fourth title, the "T.D." or Tracking Dog title, may be won at any time and tests for it are held apart from dog shows. The qualifying score is a minimum of 170 points out of a possible total of 200, with no score in any one exercise less than 50% of the points allotted.

Since the C.D. and U.D. titles are progressive, earlier titles (with the exception of the tracking titles) are dropped as a dog acquires the next higher title. If an obedience title is gained in another country in addition to the United States, that fact is signified by the word "International," followed by the title.

Effective July 1, 1977, the AKC approved the awarding of an additional title, Obedience Trial Champion (O.T. Ch.). To be eligible for this title, a dog must have earned the Utility Dog title and then must earn one hundred championship points in certain types of competition, placing First three times under different judges.

In late 1979, the Board of Directors of The American Kennel Club approved the test for the Tracking Dog Excellent (T.D.X.) title, to become effective March 1, 1980. Eligibility for this title is limited to dogs that have already earned the Tracking Dog title.

Trials for obedience trained dogs are held at most of the larger bench shows, and obedience training clubs are to be found in almost all communities today. Information concerning forthcoming trials and lists of obedience training clubs are included regularly in *Pure Bred Dogs— American Kennel Gazette* and other dog magazines. Pamphlets containing rules and regulations governing obedience competition are available upon request from The American Kennel Club, 51 Madison Avenue, New York, N.Y. 10010. Rules are revised occasionally, so if you are interested in participating in obedience competition, you should be sure your copy of the regulations is current.

All dogs must comply with the same rules, although in broad jump, high jump, and bar jump competition, the jumps are adjusted to the size of the breed. Classes at obedience trials are divided into Novice (A and B), Open (A and B), and Utility (which may be divided into A and B, at the option of the sponsoring club and with the approval of The American Kennel Club).

An ideal way to train a dog for obedience competition is to join an obedience class or a training club. In organized class work, beginners' classes cover pretty much the same exercises as those described in the chapter on manners. However, through class work you will develop greater precision than is possible in training your dog by yourself. Amateur handlers often cause the dog to be penalized, for if the handler fails to abide by the rules, it is the dog that suffers the penalty. A common infraction of the rules is using more than one signal or command where regulations stipulate only one may be used. Classwork will help eliminate such errors, which the owner may make unconsciously if he is working alone. Working with a class will also acquaint both dog and handler with ring

procedure so that obedience trials will not present unforeseen problems.

Thirty or forty owners and dogs often comprise a class, and exercises are performed in unison, with individual instruction provided if it is required. The procedure followed in training—in fact, even wording of various commands—may vary from instructor to instructor.

Dumbbells.

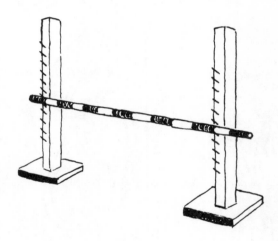

Bar jump.

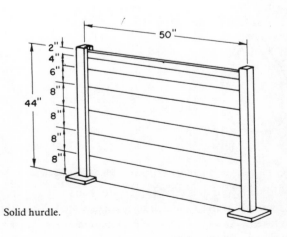

Solid hurdle.

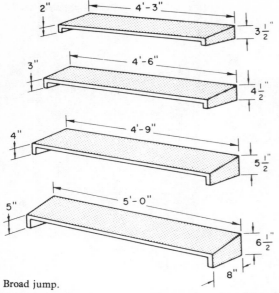

Broad jump.

Equipment used will vary somewhat, also, but will usually include a training collar and leash, a long line, a dumbbell, and a jumping stick. The latter may be a short length of heavy doweling or a broom handle and both it and the dumbbell are usually painted white for increased visibility.

A bitch in season must never be taken to a training class, so before enrolling a female dog, you should determine whether she may be expected to come into season before classes are scheduled to end. If you think she will, it is better to wait and enroll her in a later course, rather than start the course and then miss classes for several weeks.

In addition to the time devoted to actual work in class, the dog must have regular, daily training sessions for practice at home. Before each class or home training session, the dog should be exercised so he will not be highly excited when the session starts, and he must be given an opportunity to relieve himself before the session begins. (Should he have an accident during the class, it is your responsibility to clean up after him.) The dog should be fed several hours before time for the class to begin or else after the class is over—never just before going to class.

If you decide to enter your dog in obedience competition, it is well to enter a small, informal show the first time. Dogs are usually called in the order in which their names appear in the catalog, so as soon as you arrive at the show, acquaint yourself with the schedule. If your dog is not the first to be judged, spend some time at ringside, observing the routine so you will know what to expect when your dog's turn comes.

In addition to collar, leash, and other equipment, you should take your dog's food and water pans and a supply of the food and water to which he is accustomed. You should also take his brushes and combs in order to give him a last-minute brushing before you enter the ring. It is important that the dog look his best even though he isn't to be judged on his appearance.

Before entering the ring, exercise your dog, give him a drink of water, and permit him to relieve himself. Once your dog enters the ring, give him your full attention and be sure to give voice commands distinctly so he will hear and understand, for there will be many distractions at ringside.

The Novice class is for dogs that have not won the title Companion Dog. In Novice A, no person who has previously handled a dog that has won a C.D. title in the obedience ring at a licensed or member trial, and no person who has regularly trained such a dog, may enter or handle a dog. The handler must be the dog's owner or a member of the owner's immediate family. In Novice B, dogs may be handled by the owner or any other person.

The Open A class is for dogs that have won the C.D. title but have not won the C.D.X. title. Obedience judges and licensed handlers may not enter or handle dogs in this class. Each dog must be handled by the owner or by a member of his immediate family. The Open B class is for dogs that have won the title C.D. or C.D.X. A dog may continue to compete in this class after it has won the title U.D. Dogs in this class may be handled by the owner or any other person.

The Utility class is for dogs that have won the title C.D.X. Dogs that have won the title U.D. may continue to compete in this class, and dogs may be handled by the owner of any other person. Provided the AKC approves, a club may choose to divide the Utility class into Utility A and Utility B. When this is done, the Utility A class is for dogs that have won the title C.D.X. and have not won the title U.D. Obedience judges and licensed handlers may not enter or handle dogs in this class. All other dogs that are eligible for the Utility class but not eligible for Utility A may be entered in Utility B.

Novice competition includes such exercises as heeling on and off lead, the stand for examination, coming on recall, and the long sit and the long down.

In Open competition, the dog must perform such exercises as heeling free, the drop on recall, and the retrieve on the flat and over the high jump. Also, he must execute the broad jump, and the long sit and long down.

In the Utility class, competition includes scent discrimination, the directed retrieve, the signal exercise, directed jumping, and the group examination.

Tracking is the most difficult test. It is always done out-of-doors, of course, and, for obvious reasons, cannot be held at a dog show. The dog must follow a scent trail that is about a quarter mile in length. He is also required to find a scent object (glove, wallet, or other article) left by a stranger who has walked the course to lay down the scent. The dog is required to follow the trail a half to two hours after the scent is laid.

Ch. Lorahame's Roc'n Rage. Owner, Eloise Robinson (Tars Kennels). Judge, Marge Turnquist.

Ch. Stage Fire O'Ebon Will, BOB, 1978 BSCA National Specialty. Owners, Roger and Maxine Ellis (Lorgen Kennels). Photo by William Gilbert.

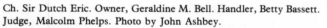

Ch. Van Mell's Command Performance. Owners, John and Marie Martin (Delting Kennels). Photo by Don Petrulis.

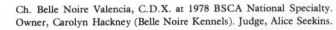

Ch. L'Ecossais Bruyere Noir. Owner, Shirley Howard (L'Ecossais Kennels).

Ch. Sir Dutch Eric. Owner, Geraldine M. Bell. Handler, Betty Bassett. Judge, Malcolm Phelps. Photo by John Ashbey.

Ch. Belle Noire Valencia, C.D.X. at 1978 BSCA National Specialty. Owner, Carolyn Hackney (Belle Noire Kennels). Judge, Alice Seekins.

The Belgian Sheepdog
at Work and Play

Ch. Esprit De Noir V. Siegestor, C.D.X., E.T., Sch-H I. Owners, Mara Lee Jiles and Rayeann Schur.

Ch. Buena Vuk of Blue Lake, C.D.X., T.D., E.T., Sch-H I. Owners, Shane and Kathay Wagoner.

The future Ch. Laddy Candide, C.D.X., at six months of age, when he completed his C.D. Owners, Robert and Barbara Krohn.

The prowess of the Belgian Sheepdog in all phases of training and work with humans—obedience, search and rescue, Schutzhund, protection, and companion dog—is not excelled by any breed.

Belgians are entering another field, sledding, which should prove most interesting. Belgian sled dog teams are making their debut in the racing circles. Their speed and lightness of foot should serve as a great asset to their success in this sport. In Alaska, Belgians are becoming recognized for their speed and for being able to adapt to extreme weather conditions because of their all-weather coats. Pulling a sled should not be too foreign to Belgians, because Belgians once pulled milk carts in their native country.

Obedience

Obedience competition is a sport that can be enjoyed by both young and old. Basic obedience training is essential for all dogs. It makes them better companions, easier to control, and the comradeship that develops between dog and trainer is a very rewarding experience for both. Obedience training is the foundation for all the other types of training that have made dogs so valuable in their service to mankind.

In obedience competition, Belgians are high-scoring dogs, and tough competitors for highest scoring dog in trial. They are willing, happy workers. Their intense desire to please makes them easy to train with the least amount of effort. They do not respond well to rough treatment and loud voice commands, which are not necessary to get the point across to them.

Belgian Sheepdogs hold more obedience titles per breed registration than the majority of dogs in the Herding and Working Groups.

Schutzhund Training

Schutzhund training and trials are comparatively new to the United States but have been popular in Europe for many years. Due perhaps to a rise in crime in the United States, this training has become more popular here. Schutzhund training is not for every person or every dog. Overaggressive or shy dogs are not recommended for training.

Schutzhund training is an extension of obedience training. It is for dedicated people who want to go on training their dogs beyond the basic obedience titles.

The first Schutzhund trial in the United States was held in 1969-1970. Belgian Sheepdogs placed first and second in the competition.

A dog that has won his degrees in an official Schutzhund trial is a well-trained family pet that will do equally well in the obedience ring, in tracking, in search and rescue, and in defense of his owner, family, and home. The dog has to have a sound, stable temperament to go through the training necessary for him to reach his full potential as a working dog.

There are a number of Schutzhund clubs in the United States presently, but they do not offer their training to the general public, as the obedience clubs do. The Schutzhund clubs are for members only.

The Schutzhund I, II, and III degrees, as recognized worldwide, each consist of three parts: A—Tracking, B—Obedience, and C—Protection. Each of the three sections are scored on a scale of 100 points, for a possible total score of 300. In order to pass the test, the dog must score at least 70 points in the A and B sections and at least 80 points in the C section. The dog must earn the Schutzhund I degree before proceeding to Schutzhund II competition. As each successive degree is earned, the previous degree is dropped and the new degree added behind the dog's name.

The rules governing Schutzhund trials are set forth by the North American Working Dog Association (NASA), an independent, non-profit organization established under the rules of the World Dog Federation (Federation Cynologique Internationale, or FCI), with headquarters in Belgium. NASA maintains that a dog is only as beautiful as it is functional. To perform properly, the dog must be both mentally and anatomically correct.

Schutzhund I

Schutzhund I is the first level for a protection-trained dog. The dog must be fourteen months or older and must pass a temperament test before he can enter Schutzhund competition.

In the Tracking section, the dog must follow an

Above and below: Mex. and Am. Ch. and O.T. Ch. Windstorm V. Siegestor, T.D., P.C., E.T., A.T.D., Int. Sch-H III Ch., pictured in Schutzhund training. Owner, Kurt Marti.

Mex. and Am. Ch. Condor V. Siegestor, U.D.T., P.C., E.T., A.T.D., Sch-H III. Owner, Kathy Marti.

Schutzhund Trial winners, 1980: Left to right, Mex. and Am. Ch. and O.T. Ch. Windstorm V. Siegestor, T.D., P.C., E.T., A.T.D., Int. Sch-H III Ch. Owner, Kurt Marti; Zorro V. Siegestor, C.D.X., E.T., Sch-H II. Owner, Robin Smiley; Mex. and Am. Ch. Condor V. Siegestor, U.D.T., P.C., E.T., A.T.D., Sch-H III. Owner, Kathy Marti; Ch. Esprit De Noir V. Siegestor, C.D.X., E.T., Sch-H I. Owners, Mara Lee Jiles and Rayeann Schur; Ch. Bando V. Siegestor, C.D., T.D., E.T., A.T.D. Owners, Mara Lee Jiles and Rayeann Schur.

unmarked track of at least 400 paces while on a twenty-foot lead. The track must be at least twenty minutes old and have two turns. The track is laid by the dog's own handler. Two articles are dropped which the dog must locate.

The Obedience section includes basic heeling on and off leash, and walking through a group of people. A gun is fired when the dog is off leash, and the dog will fail the trial if he is gun-shy. The dog must obey sit and down commands while heeling, as the handler continues on. On the sit command, the handler returns to the dog. On the down command, the dog will be called to the handler. Another exercise is a retrieve over a thirty-nine inch jump; the dog must retrieve the article. The final exercise is the long down-stay, with the handler some distance away with his back to the dog. The dog remains in the down-stay position while another dog completes its exercises.

In the Protection section, a human decoy hides in a field and the dog must locate him. The dog must bark but not bite. Next, the dog, heeling off lead, must attack the decoy, who will come out of hiding to attack the dog's handler. The decoy will hit the dog with a switch, and the dog must not show fear. On command, the dog must stop his aggression. The decoy then runs away, acting in a belligerent manner, and the handler sends the dog after him to attack and hold.

Schutzhund II

A dog must pass Schutzhund I before attempting the requirements for the Schutzhund II degree. The three sections are the same.

In Tracking, the dog must find two lost articles over a strange trail, about 600 paces long and at least thirty minutes old, while on an eleven-yard-long lead. The trail will have two turns.

The first part of the Obedience section is the same as in Schutzhund I: heeling on and off lead, proof of not being gun-shy, and a sit-stay and down-stay. Three other exercises test the dog's retrieving ability. In the first exercise, the dog retrieves a 2.2 pound wooden dumbbell over level ground. In the second, the dog retrieves a 1.7 pound wooden dumbbell with a free jump over a forty-inch hurdle. In the third, the dog is required to go over a sixty-four-inch jump and retrieve an object belonging to his handler. The dog must execute a "go-away," leaving his handler, on command, for at least thirty paces in a fast gait in an indicated direction, and must lie down on command. This is followed by the long down stay, with the handler some distance away with his back to the dog. The dog remains in this position while another dog completes its exercises.

In the Protection section, the dog must first locate the decoy hiding in a field. He must bark but not bite. The handler leaves the dog to guard the "suspect" while he investigates the suspect's hiding place. The suspect then tries to escape and the dog must stop him by seizing him. When the suspect stops trying to escape, the dog must stop his aggression without command. The suspect then tries to attack the dog with a stick, and the dog must immediately attack the suspect to prevent him from further aggression. Next, the suspect is transported with the dog and handler about forty paces behind. After the transport, the suspect will attempt to attack the handler, and the dog must prevent the attack. In the courage exercise, the dog is sent after the suspect, who is about fifty paces away. The dog must seize the suspect and hold him firmly until called off by his handler.

Schutzhund III

This is the most advanced Schutzhund degree. The sections are the same as in Schutzhund I and II.

In Tracking, the dog must search for three lost articles on a track approximately 1,200 paces long and at least fifty minutes old. The dog may be worked off lead or on an eleven-yard-long lead.

In Obedience, exercises similar to those in I and II are used, with the addition of two exercises which require the dog to stand on command from a walk and from a run. The handler returns to the dog. In other exercises, the dog must retrieve a 4.4 pound dumbbell over flat ground, and complete a free jump with a 1.7 pound dumbbell over a forty-inch jump, and climb a seventy-one-inch-high wall. The "go away" is similar to the Schutzhund II exercise, except that the dog must go away from his handler forty paces. The last exercise is the long down-stay with the handler fifty feet away, out of sight of his dog.

In the Protection section, the exercises are much the same as in Schutzhund II. The dog chases a suspect who strikes the dog, and the dog must subdue and hold the suspect. The dog is scored on his over-all combativeness during the protection portion of this test.

Endurance Test

The test for the endurance degree (E.T. or A.D.) requires that the dog exert physical effort without exhibiting extreme fatigue. The test is held on roads and paths of as many different surfaces as possible, for a distance of 12.4 miles. There are three rest stops, at which the dogs are checked by a judge for signs of fatigue or other problems.

To be eligible for the test, a dog must be at least twelve months old, and be in good health and physical condition. The dog is on leash and must gait at a speed of about 6.2 miles per hour on the right side of the handler. The handler may run or ride a bicycle. The dog, on a loose lead, is allowed to pull forward but is not allowed to lag behind for any length of time. When half of the distance has been covered, there is a ten minute rest period.

The judge must follow the dog the entire distance and must be present at the rest period. A car is available to pick up any dog that is unable to complete the full distance.

A fifteen minute break follows the completion of the running, and then the dog must exhibit basic obedience work, including off lead heeling and a retrieve of a dumbbell or object over a thirty-nine-inch jump.

If a dog lacks temper or toughness, shows signs of exceptional fatigue and/or cannot keep up a speed of six miles per hour, the examination is considered "not passed." Two hours are allowed for the completion of the endurance examination.

Search and Rescue

Search and rescue training covers many phases of humanitarian endeavor. Dogs are trained to rescue victims of earthquakes, tornadoes, and avalanches, and to find persons lost in rural or wilderness areas.

We all have read in newspapers of dogs being used to search in rubble and debris for victims of a disaster. The dogs' keen hearing and sense of smell can direct them to victims who would be overlooked by human searchers. Many lives have been saved by courageous trainers and their dogs.

Much of the training is based on an extension of obedience exercises. The trainer has to have complete control of his dog at all times. The obedience exercises used for this work are on-leash and off-leash heeling, the direct-go or send-out exercise, scent discrimination, and the long down-stay with the handler out of sight.

The dogs are taught to crawl through openings, to proceed with caution, and to be alert to unstable debris and terrain. When a victim is located, the dog must alert his handler and stay in place until help arrives.

Avalanche dogs were first developed in Austria, and the first dogs to be used for this work were Belgian Sheepdogs. In avalanche rescue work, the dog has to search in ice and snow. When he finds a victim, he will start to dig. His sense of smell is so keen that he can detect a body covered with snow and debris. The handler and the dog must be in good physical condition and have a close relationship. The

Isadora V. Siegestor tracking at ten weeks. Owners, Robin and Sarah Smiley and Kurt Marti.

dog has to have a stable, sound temperament to go through the rigorous training necessary for this work.

There are groups of people in America who have organized to train their dogs toward the goal of being ready to help in any search and rescue emergency.

The average working life span of a rescue dog is eight years. It takes months of training to qualify for search and rescue work. Since adult dogs have but a few years to work after completion of their training, advocates of this type of work have started training their future search and rescue dogs as young as eight weeks. The training is begun in easy stages, with plenty of socialization with people and other dogs, riding in cars, and being exposed to new situations and places that will give the dogs confidence and allow them to adapt to change and noise which they will encounter in later training.

Basic obedience can be introduced at this point, with the dog learning to walk on lead, to sit on command, and to come when called. This training requires patience, and lots of praise when the dog responds. Tracking can be fun for the puppy as he learns to use his nose to find his handler, concealed a short distance away. The reward should be lots of praise, and a good romp together. The distance should be increased gradually, and other members of the family can be included in this game.

Learning to walk across unstable boards is another part of training, and can be frightening to a puppy. The handler should never push the puppy, but should give him voice encouragement and pet him when he takes some steps forward. When he makes it across, the praise should be lavish, with plenty of petting. If the puppy gets that much attention, he will be willing to try it again. He will soon get his "sea legs," and another obstacle will have been surmounted. A puppy is naturally curious, which makes learning and adapting to new situations much easier for him than for an adult dog.

Search and rescue work is the most physically and mentally demanding of all the services rendered by a handler and his dog for mankind. Catastrophes do not happen at a convenient time or place. Rescue teams may be called to go by helicopter to mountainous areas that cannot be reached by foot. The rescuers have to be ready to go by any conveyance that is available, often under severe climatic conditions, and work for hours or days at a stretch to accomplish their mission. They are unsung heroes, unpaid volunteers who subject themselves and their dogs to the hardships they endure. Their only reward is in finding a missing person who would have perished without their help, and the gratitude of the families and friends of the victims.

Ch. Greenfield's Fleur De Lys, C.D.X., Sch-H I, S.H., K.H. Owners, Bill and Carolyn Dotson.

Herding

Belgian Sheepdogs have an instinct for herding. They were originally bred as herding dogs and have excelled in this field of endeavor for many years in Europe. A Mr. de Corte, who bred Belgians about 1917, wrote an article about his grandparents in Flanders. Long before there were railroads between Flanders and Belgium, all the cattle and sheep raised in Flanders had to travel on foot to the Belgian markets. The black Groenendael-type sheepdogs were the only guardians of the flocks, generally with but one man in charge over them. They were always faithful and reliable in their duties, and indispensable in moving cattle and sheep across the wild, rough terrain.

Belgian Sheepdogs have very sensitive hearing and are alert to any noise that could mean harm to their charges. They have speed and a fast takeoff, and they are so agile that they can reverse directions to turn back strays without losing speed.

There are unsubstantiated stories of Belgians herding great flocks of sheep, which always travel very close together, and which would become frightened by wild animals and start a stampede. It is said that Belgians have run across the backs of the sheep and will drop down in front of the flock to stop the panic-stricken animals.

The Belgian has either an even or a scissor bite. The even bite is an asset in herding. Sometimes the dog has to nip its charges to get them moving, and the even bite will pinch but not tear the skin. The scissor bite, on the other hand, can be beneficial in protection work, for holding more securely.

Many people in the United States are becoming aware of the herding ability of Belgians. They are being used to herd many different animals, including ducks, geese, and turkeys. Sometimes the Belgians' inbred instinct for herding gets them into trouble for herding things that some people do not want herded. I know of some young Belgian pups that escaped from their fenced-in yard, went over to a neighboring rancher's spread, rounded up his cattle, put them in the cattle lot, and would not let them out. The charade ended when the dogs' owners were called and the culprits were relieved of their unsolicited efforts at being helpful neighbors.

At the present time, there is no official herding title. Belgian fanciers have held herding seminars and trials, but no official tests have been established.

Ch. Buena Vuk of Blue Lake, C.D.X., T.D., E.T., Sch-H I. Owners, Shane and Kathay Wagoner.

Ch. Greenfield's Fleur De Lys, C.D.X., Sch-H I, S.H., K.H. Owners, Bill and Carolyn Dotson. Callea Photo.

Ch. Thunder Cloud V. Siegestor. Owner, Alan Molchan. Callea Photo.

"Fun and Games." Rear: Belle Noire Laxson du Jet. Front, left to right: Grand Fond Amazone Noire, Grand Fond Aigle Noire, and Voudoun's Pagan Jona An, C.D. Owner, Kaye Hall.

Belgian Sheepdogs at Play

Belgian Sheepdogs have a pixyish sense of humor. If you yourself do not have this attribute, then you will not appreciate this trait in Belgians. They are alert to any situation that will give them a chance to play a prank on their unsuspecting owner. They enjoy all types of games and enter into them with enthusiasm and fervor. They love to swim, play in snow, retrieve objects, go jogging with their owners, catch frisbees, or be involved in any game that requires physical dexterity.

Belgians adapt well to people who may not be as active, however. They are sensitive to the moods of their people and respond with gentle understanding. They love children and children's games but also are reliable as guardians for small children. Their intelligence and adaptability makes them all-around family dogs.

Am. and Can. Ch. Jaye's Von Jet stars in the musical "George M" at the Boarshead Theater. Owner, Elaine Jaye.

Ch. Voudoun's Ethiopian Wolf, C.D., and her son Ch. Voudoun's Rowdy Wolf, C.D. Owners, Margery and Jon Riddle.

60

BREED RECORDS

First Champion: Either King Cole (Owner, Harry Weatherby) or Ajax (imported from Holland by Mrs. G. M. Soetor). (1920s)

First American and Canadian Champion: Am. and Can. Ch. Uhlan Bar Bingen, U.D.T., Can. C.D.X. Owner, Mary Dillaway. (1961)

First American and English Champion: Am. and Eng. Ch. Laralee's Traveler. Owner, Doreen Bushby (England). (1971)

First Group Placement: Philmont Boy. Owner, Mrs. Jno K. Curran. (1933)

First Group I Placement: Ch. Flicky Candide, C.D. Owner, Dorothea Kelley. (1959)

First Companion Dog Excellent: Ch. Hadji de Flanders, U.D.T. Owner, Clara Vestal. (1940s)

First Companion Dog Excellent (Bitch): Dianne de Beaute Noir, C.D.X. Owner, Art Brindel. (1949)

First Utility Dog: Ch. Hadji de Flanders, U.D.T. Owner, Clara Vestal. (1947)

First Utility Dog (Bitch): Sheba III de Beaute Noir, U.D. Owner, Rudy Robinson. (1950)

First Utility Dog Tracking: Ch. Hadji de Flanders, U.D.T. Owner, Clara Vestal. (1948)

First Utility Dog Tracking (Bitch): Ch. A'Dew Skipon Rebel O'Ebon Will, U.D.T. Owner, Stephanie Jay Price. (1981)

First Companion Dog Tracking (Bitch): Vicki Carobingen, C.D., T.D. Owner, Rita Catsby. (1963)

First Obedience Trial Champion: Windstorm V. Siegestor, T.D., P.C., E.T., A.T.D., INT. Sch-H III Ch. Owner-Breeder, Kurt Marti. (1979)

First Schutzhund I Champion: Am. and Mex. Ch. Bruce V Kaiserhof, Sch-H III. Owner, Kurt Marti. (1970)

First Schutzhund I Champion (Bitch): Ch. Laralee's Personality, C.D., Sch-H I. Owner, Pat Crabtree. (1974)

First Schutzhund II Champion: Ch. Fireball V. Siegestor, U.D., Sch-H III. Owner, Elaine Hornbuckle. (1971)

First Schutzhund III Champion: Am. and Mex. Ch. Bruce V Kaiserhof, Sch-H III. Owner, Kurt Marti. (1972)

First AD: Am. and Mex. Ch. Rafer V Siegestor, U.D., Sch-H I, A.D. Owner, Elaine Hornbuckle. (1972)

First Triple Champion Bitch: Am., Mex., and Can. Ch. Johnsondale's High-Mount Indigo. Owner, Pat Johnson. (1978)

First Group Winner: Ch. Dianne de Beaute Noir, C.D.X. Owner, Mr. and Mrs. Arthur Brindel.(Late 1940s)

First Best in Show winner: Am. and Can. Ch. Skip's Reward O'Ebon Will. Owner, Mrs. William Hendricks. (1973)

The first Obedience Trial Champion of the breed: Mex. and Am. Ch. & O.T. Ch. Windstorm V. Siegestor, T.D., P.C., E.T., A.T.D., Int. Sch-H III Ch. Breeder-Owner, Kurt Marti.

First E.T. (or A.D.): Am. and Mex. Ch. Rafer V Siegestor, U.D., Sch-H I, A.D. Owner, Elaine Hornbuckle. (1972)

First Belgian Sheepdog Best in Show winner, and BOB at 1972 and 1973 BSCA National Specialties. Am. and Can. Ch. Skip's Reward O'Ebon Will. (Ch. Stage Hand O'Ebon Will, C.D. x Ch. Banjoette O'Ebon Will, U.D.) Owner, Terry Hendricks.

Ch. Zita de L'Infernal. (You de L'Infernal x Via de L'Infernal.) Owner, Rudy Robinson.

Ch. Pandora of Geier Tal, BOS, 1963 BSCA National Specialty. (Fier Beaute Noir x Ch. Laurel of Geier Tal.) Owners, Marge and Ed Turnquist.

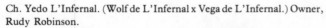

Ch. Yedo L'Infernal. (Wolf de L'Infernal x Vega de L'Infernal.) Owner, Rudy Robinson.

Ch. Laurel of Geier Tal, BOS at the 1957 BSCA National Specialty. (Ch. Zulvo, C.D., x Ch. Liza del Pirata Nero, C.D.) Owners, Marge and Ed Turnquist.

Ch. Black Prince. (Lloyd's Little Nero of Bel-Peke x Roll in Fancy.) Owner, Carol Gerber.

History of the Genus Canis

The history of man's association with the dog is a fascinating one, extending into the past at least seventy centuries, and involving the entire history of civilized man from the early Stone Age to the present.

The dog, technically a member of the genus *Canis*, belongs to the zoological family group *Canidae*, which also includes such animals as wolves, foxes, jackals, and coyotes. In the past it was generally agreed that the dog resulted from the crossing of various members of the family *Canidae*. Recent findings have amended this theory somewhat, and most authorities now feel the jackal probably has no direct relationship with the dog. Some believe dogs are descended from wolves and foxes, with the wolf the main progenitor. As evidence, they cite the fact that the teeth of the wolf are identical in every detail with those of the dog, whereas the teeth of the jackal are totally different.

Still other authorities insist that the dog always has existed as a separate and distinct animal. This group admits that it is possible for a dog to mate with a fox, coyote, or wolf, but points out that the resulting puppies are unable to breed with each other, although they can breed with stock of the same genus as either parent. Therefore, they insist, it was impossible for a new and distinct genus to have developed from such crossings. They then cite the fact that any dog can be mated with any other dog and the progeny bred among themselves. These researchers point out, too, heritable characteristics that are different in these animals. For instance, the pupil of the eye of the fox is eliptical and vertical, while the pupil is round in the dog, wolf, and coyote. Tails, too, differ considerably, for tails of foxes, coyotes, and wolves always drop behind them, while those of dogs may be carried over the back or straight up.

Much conjecture centers on two wild dog species that still exist—the Dingo of Australia, and the Dhole in India. Similar in appearance, both are reddish in color, both have rather long, slender jaws, both have rounded ears that stand straight up, and both species hunt in packs. Evidence indicates that they had the same ancestors. Yet, today, they live in areas that are more than 4,000 miles apart.

Despite the fact that it is impossible to determine just when the dog first appeared as a distinct species, archeologists have found definite proof that the dog was the first animal domesticated by man. When man lived by tracking, trapping, and killing game, the dog added to the forces through which man discovered and captured the quarry. Man shared his primitive living quarters with the dog, and the two together devoured the prey. Thus, each

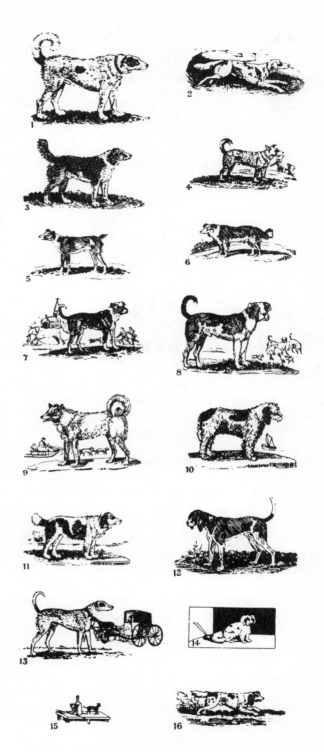

1. The Newfoundland. 2. The English Setter. 3. The Large Water-Spaniel. 4. The Terrier. 5. The Cur-dog. 6. The Shepherd's Dog. 7. The Bulldog. 8. The Mastiff. 9. The Greenland Dog. 10. The Rough-Water-dog. 11. The Small Water-Spaniel. 12. The Old English Hound. 13. The Dalmatian or Coach-dog. 14. The Comporter (very much of a Papillon). 15. "Toy Dog, Bottle, Glass, and Pipe." *From a vignette.* 16. The Springer or Cocker. *From Thomas Bewick's "General History of Quadrapeds" (1790).*

"Spotted sporting dog trained to catch game."

"Mad dog of Grevinus."

"Spanish dog with floppy ears."

Dogs in Woodcuts, above, from Aldrovandus (1637).

The Stone-Age Dog.

Spotted Dog from India, "Parent of the modern Coach Dog."

helped to sustain the life of the other. The dog assisted man, too, by defending the campsite against marauders. As man gradually became civilized, the dog's usefulness was extended to guarding the other animals man domesticated, and, even before the wheel was invented, the dog served as a beast of burden. In fact, archeological findings show that aboriginal peoples of Switzerland and Ireland used the dog for such purposes long before they learned to till the soil.

Cave drawings from the palaeolithic era, which was the earliest part of the Old World Stone Age, include hunting scenes in which a rough, canine-like form is shown alongside huntsmen. One of these drawings is believed to be 50,000 years old, and gives credence to the theory that all dogs are descended from a primitive type ancestor that was neither fox nor wolf.

Archeological findings show that Europeans of the New Stone Age possessed a breed of dogs of wolf-like appearance, and a similar breed has been traced through the successive Bronze Age and Iron Age. Accurate details are not available, though, as to the external appearance of domesticated dogs prior to historic times (roughly four to five thousand years ago).

Early records in Chaldean and Egyptian tombs show that several distinct and well-established dog types had been developed by about 3700 B.C. Similar records show that the early people of the Nile Valley regarded the dog as a god, often burying it as a mummy in special cemeteries and mourning its death.

Some of the early Egyptian dogs had been given names, such as Akna, Tarn, and Abu, and slender dogs of the

Greyhound type and a short-legged Terrier type are depicted in drawings found in Egyptian royal tombs that are at least 5,000 years old. The Afghan Hound and the Saluki are shown in drawings of only slightly later times. Another type of ancient Egyptian dog was much heavier and more powerful, with short coat and massive head. These probably hunted by scent, as did still another type of Egyptian dog that had a thick furry coat, a tail curled almost flat over the back, and erect "prick" ears.

Early Romans and Greeks mentioned their dogs often in literature, and both made distinctions between those that hunted by sight and those that hunted by scent. The Romans' canine classifications were similar to those we use now. In addition to dogs comparable to the Greek sight and scent hounds, the ancient Romans had Canes *villatici* (housedogs) and Canes *pastorales* (sheepdogs), corresponding to our present-day working dogs.

The dog is mentioned many times in the Old Testament. The first reference, in Genesis, leads some Biblical scholars to assert that man and dog have been companions from the time man was created. And later Biblical references bring an awareness of the diversity in breeds and types existing thousands of years ago.

As civilization advanced, man found new uses for dogs. Some required great size and strength. Others needed less of these characteristics but greater agility and better sight. Still others needed an accentuated sense of smell. As time went on, men kept those puppies that suited specific purposes especially well and bred them together. Through ensuing generations of selective breeding, desirable characteristics appeared with increasing frequency. Dogs

Am. and Can. Ch. Mi-Sha-Ook's Wonita. (John Du Mas De Sevre x Ch. Mi-Sha-Ook's Juliano Paola.) BOS at the 1980 BSCA National Specialty. Owner, Marcella Spalding.

Ch. Coaltree's Texas Spitfire, C.D., A.D. (Wildfire At Coaltree, C.D., A.D., x Ch. Laralee's Personality, C.D.X., Sch-H I, A.D.) BOS at the 1981 BSCA National Specialty. Owner, Anita Meeks.

Ch. Chip Harbe, Esq., and Love Bug O'Litland, Best of Breed and Best of Opposite Sex, May 6, 1979, at the Redwood Empire Show. Owners-handlers, Millard and Jeani Brown.

"Maltese dog with shorter hair."

"Sporting white dog."

"Hairy Maltese dog."

"French dog."

Dogs in Woodcuts.
From Aldrovandus (1637).

"English fighting dog . . . of horrid aspect."

used in a particular region for a special purpose gradually became more like each other, yet less like dogs of other areas used for different purposes. Thus were established the foundations for the various breeds we have today.

The American Kennel Club, the leading dog organization in the United States, divides the various breeds into seven "Groups," based on similarity of purposes for which they were developed.

"Sporting Dogs" include the Pointers, Setters, Spaniels, and Retrievers that were developed by sportsmen interested in hunting game birds. Most of the Pointers and Setters are of comparatively recent origin. Their development parallels the development of sporting firearms, and most of them evolved in the British Isles. Exceptions are the Weimaraner, which was developed in Germany, and the Vizsla, or Hungarian Pointer, believed to have been developed by the Magyar hordes that swarmed over Central Europe a thousand years ago. The Irish were among the first to use Spaniels, though the name indicates that the original stock may have come from Spain. Two Sporting breeds, the American Water Spaniel and the Chesapeake Bay Retriever, were developed entirely in the United States.

"Hounds," among which are Dachshunds, Beagles, Bassets, Harriers, and Foxhounds, are used singly, in pairs, or in packs to "course" (or run) and hunt for rabbits, foxes, and various rodents. But little larger, the Norwegian Elkhound is used in its native country to hunt big game—moose, bear, and deer.

The smaller Hound breeds hunt by scent, while the Irish Wolfhound, Borzoi, Scottish Deerhound, Saluki, and Greyhound hunt by sight. The Whippet, Saluki, and Greyhound are notably fleet of foot, and racing these breeds (particularly the Greyhound) is popular sport.

The Bloodhound is a member of the Hound Group that is known world-wide for its scenting ability. On the other hand, the Basenji is a comparatively rare Hound breed and has the distinction of being the only dog that cannot bark.

Until January 1, 1983, "Working Dogs" included eighteen breeds currently in that Group, as well as fifteen breeds now in the "Herding" Group. The Working Dogs have great utilitarian value and contribute to man's welfare in diverse ways. The Boxer, Doberman Pinscher, Rottweiler, Great Dane, and Giant Schnauzer often are trained to serve as sentries and aid police in patrolling streets. The exploits of the Saint Bernard and Newfoundland are legendary, their records for saving lives unsurpassed.

The Siberian Husky, the Samoyed, and the Alaskan Malamute are noted for tremendous strength and stamina. Had it not been for these hardy Northern breeds, the great polar expeditions might never have taken place, for Admiral Byrd used these dogs to reach points inaccessible by other means. Even today, with our jet-age transportation, the Northern breeds provide a more practical means of travel in frigid areas than do modern machines.

"Terriers" derive their name from the Latin *terra*, meaning "earth," for all of the breeds in this group are fond of burrowing. Terriers hunt by digging into the earth to rout rodents and fur-bearing animals such as badgers, woodchucks, and otters. Some breeds are expected merely to force the animals from their dens in order that the hunter can complete the capture. Others are expected to find and destroy the prey, either on the surface or under the ground.

Terriers come in a wide variety of sizes, ranging from such large breeds as the Airedale and Kerry Blue to such small ones as the Skye, the Dandie Dinmont, the West Highland White, and the Scottish Terrier. England, Ireland, and Scotland produced most of the Terrier breeds, although the Miniature Schnauzer was developed in Germany.

"Toys," as the term indicates, are small breeds. Although they make little claim to usefulness other than as ideal housepets, Toy dogs develop as much protective instinct as do larger breeds and serve effectively in warning of the approach of strangers.

Origins of the Toys are varied. The Pekingese was developed as the royal dog of China more than two thousand years before the birth of Christ. The Chihuahua, smallest of the Toys, originated in Mexico and is believed to be a descendant of the Techichi, a dog of great religious significance to the Aztecs, while the Italian Greyhound was popular in the days of ancient Pompeii.

"Non-Sporting Dogs" include a number of popular breeds of varying ancestry. The Standard and Miniature Poodles were developed in France for the purpose of retrieving game from water. The Bulldog originated in Great Britain and was bred for the purpose of "baiting" bulls. The Chow Chow apparently originated centuries ago in China, for it is pictured in a bas relief dated to the Han dynasty of about 150 B.C.

The Dalmatian served as a carriage dog in Dalmatia, protecting travelers in bandit-infested regions. The Keeshond, recognized as the national dog of Holland, is believed to have originated in the Arctic or possibly the Sub-Arctic. The Schipperke, sometimes erroneously described as a Dutch dog, originated in the Flemish provinces of Belgium. And the Lhasa Apso came from Tibet, where it is known as "Abso Seng Kye," the "Bark Lion Sentinel Dog."

The breeds in the "Herding" Group are known throughout the world for their extraordinary ability as herders of sheep, cattle, and other animals. Some show their abilities by "herding" children who might otherwise come to harm, and the German Shepherd is noted especially as a guide dog for the blind. In the Herding Group are the three breeds of Collies, the various breeds of Sheepdogs, and the two Corgi breeds.

During the thousands of years that man and dog have been closely associated, a strong affinity has been built up between the two. The dog has more than earned his way as

Bas-relief of Assyrian Mastiffs hunting wild horses. *British Museum.*

a helper, and his faithful, selfless devotion to man is legendary. The ways in which the dog has proved his intelligence, his courage, and his dependability in situations of stress are amply recorded in the countless tales of canine heroism that highlight the pages of history, both past and present.

Bas-relief of Hunters with Nets and Mastiffs. From the walls of Assurbanipal's palace at Nineveh 668-626 B.C. *British Museum.*

First Companion Dog Excellent, Utility Dog, and Utility Dog Tracking: Ch. Hadji de Flanders, U.D.T., with owner Clara Vestal.

First American and Canadian champion: Am. and Can. Ch. Uhlan Bar Bingen, U.D.T., Can. C.D.X. (Ch. Yedo de L'Infernal x Ch. Barbi Candide, C.D.X.) Owner, Mary Dillaway.

The Story of the Belgian Sheepdog

The lineage of the Belgian Sheepdog can be traced back to Central Europe, and in particular to the Mooreland dog. The breed was considered the national dog of Belgium, and some believe, inspired Quida's *Dog of Flanders,* and the more famous poet, philosopher, and dramatist Maeterlinck's *Our Friend the Dog.*

In 1897, the history of the Groenendael (long-haired black) Belgian Sheepdog began. A resident of Uccle, Mr. Bernaerts, had found a Belgian Shepherd dog with long black hair, working as a herd dog in Feluy-Arguennes. He was impressed by its beauty, speed, and gentleness in herding the flock. He acquired the dog and named him Piccard D'Uccle. N. Rose, proprietor of the Restaurant du Chateau de Groenendael, had already been successful in breeding several Belgian Shepherds, as they were called at that time, with long black hair, and he owned a bitch called Petite. She was bred to Mr. Bernaerts's black dog Piccard D'Uccle and produced Duc de Groenendael, a fine specimen in every way, with beautiful small ears and good tail carriage, but with a large white marking on his chest. From the same litter came Pitt, Baronne, Margot, and Bergere, all with the suffix "of Groenendael," and it was in this manner that the kennel name became the name of one of the types of Belgian Sheepdogs. All of our good Groenendaels are descendants of these dogs. Piccard D'Uccle was interbred very heavily to his offspring; evidently the breeders were trying to establish type and coat color.

Groenendaels became quite a vogue. Before World War I Belgian fanciers were enthusiastic about the black dogs, and at shows there generally were entries of one hundred or more Groenendael specimens. The war curtailed the breeding program enormously. The serious breeders kept some of their best breeding stock, but bred fewer litters. The requests for imports became so great that they could not accommodate all of them. The European breeders did not succumb to the lure of money and continued to produce comparatively few, but constantly fine, Groenendaels.

During World War I, the Groenendaels filled many important posts. During the fighting in Belgium and France they were used on the battlefield to search for injured soldiers and to convey messages from place to place. The black coat proved to be perfect camouflage for traveling at night without detection. They were alert companions in the trenches and their faithfulness, obedience, and amiability endeared them to all who depended on them.

The exact year that the first imports came to North America is not known, but the first Belgians registered by the AKC were imported by Josse Hanssens of Norwalk, Connecticut, in 1911. They were first registered as "German Sheepdogs." These were two Groenendaels, Belgian Dora des Remparts and Belgian Duke, and two listed as Auburn, probably of the Malinois type, Ch. Belgian Blackie and Belgian Mouche. L. I. de Winter produced the first Groenendael litter in America in 1912. Two of the offspring listed are Belgian King Cole (black) and Winterview Dox (black and white).

About the year 1914, there were six Groenendaels in the kennels of a Belgian immigrant on Staten Island, Auguste de Corte. Harry Weatherby, of Englewood, New Jersey, owned Ch. King Cole, a dog that figured conspicuously in the early history of the breed, not only for his show honors, but for his valuable service to the Englewood police. These two men were active in the promotion of the breed in that era.

During this period there seemed to be a lack of selective breeding, and many mediocre progeny were in evidence. A Mr. M. George Domus of Canada sensed the need for better producers and sent money to Belgium to Joseph M. Panesi of Antwerp for the procurement of some good, producing Belgians. In 1921 Mr. Domus came into possession of a dog and bitch, Galopin and Netty, the best of their respective strains. The mating of these two was impressive enough to establish the prediction that Mr. Domus would be known as the founder of the Groenendael type on the American continent. Galopin and Netty produced Ch. Jet, Ch. Marco, Ch. Pearl of Belgium, and other progeny. Evidently they were very dominant in their genetic traits, because dogs descended from these two show similar characteristics.

In a 1917 issue of the magazine *Dogdom,* there was a picture of a Groenendael Sheepdog, Ajax, owned by a Mrs. G. M. Soeter, of Brooklyn, New York. This dog was whelped July 28, 1915, in Amsterdam, Holland, and was imported by Mrs. Soeter in 1916. This dog was absolutely black and was twenty-six inches in height. He was shown once in Holland and continued to be shown in the United States, winning two Firsts, Winners, and one Special at Grant City in April 1917, and two Firsts and Winners at the Brooklyn, Long Island Kennel Club Show, May 30, 1917. Ajax finished his championship and would be a tough competitor in the ring today.

H. A. Ghislain and his family, natives of Belgium, came to America in 1913. At that time, commercial embargoes prevented importation of dogs, and the laws of

Holiday Florimel of Ganymede and the Couter family won first prize in 1964 Labor Day Parade. Owner, Mary Courter.

A del Pirata Nero dog from Italy giving an exhibition. Owner, Angelo Colombo.

Pennsylvania, where Mr. Ghislain became a resident, forbade him, a foreign subject, even to own one. It was not until 1921, when Mrs. Ghislain traveled to Belgium on a visit and returned with four Groenendaels, two grown dogs and two puppies, that the family again felt complete with their much-loved Belgians. They moved to Shreveport, Louisiana, but tragedy struck them on the way when one of their adult dogs, a son of Piratin de L'enfer, was killed by a car while exercising by the roadside. The Ghislains reached their destination and while looking for a country location they rented city property. Unfortunately they had unfriendly neighbors who disliked dogs, and the neighbors killed the other adult dog. Mr. Ghislain took his case to court, in the vain hope of obtaining redress. He was informed that the law recognized no intrinsic value in the life of a mere dog. Broken-hearted but undaunted over their loss, the Ghislains found some isolated farm land and moved with their remaining two dogs to a safe refuge where they bred and raised many fine Groenendaels that were a credit to the breed. Mr. Ghislain became a naturalized citizen of the United States and became a member of the first Belgian Sheepdog Club of America. I have seen pictures of some of the Ghislains' dogs in an old magazine, and I believe those dogs do not look any different from the dogs being shown today, and perhaps even look better.

These are just a few of the pioneers of the breed and there are many, many more that were important in the breeding programs and in the development of the breed. Most of their stories will never be told because much of the information and many pictures have been destroyed with the demise of the original Belgian enthusiasts. Each dog in an old pedigree has a poignant story behind its existence, along with the hopes and dreams of its owners and breeders. Some breeders were successful, others dropped out, but all of them contributed something to introducing an unknown breed to the public. It would be interesting to know how these dogs found their way to so many dog shows across the country in the time before there was any organized breed club.

Looking back through some old show catalogs of Phyllis Green, a senior member of our local Mid-Continent Kennel Club of Tulsa, Oklahoma, we found that a Belgian Sheepdog was entered in a 1925 show. The dog's name was Commerca. (Breeder, M. M. Bruen. Listed June 25, 1919. Owner, G. Lynn Rohrback.)

In 1925, at Waco, Texas, two Belgians were entered: One was Brussels, by Liege x Loraine of Belgian. (Breeder, H. H. Johanning, Phoenix, Arizona. Listed September 8, 1924. Owner, V. J. Zienter.) A litter mate was entered and offered for sale for $150.00.

In 1927, in Oklahoma City, Oklahoma, there was one Belgian entered in three classes, Puppy Dog, Novice, and Open: this was Rene de Lorrona, by Porthos Deshorrona

ex Lady Delenfer. (Breeder, Don Shaffer. Listed March 6. 1927. Owner, Irene Wood.)

In 1932 at the Tulsa Mid-Continent Show, a bitch, Princess Riska, by Fidac ex Charlott, was entered in the Open Class. (Breeder, Mrs. Frank Phillips of Phillips Petroleum in Bartlesville, Oklahoma. Listed October 30, 1930. Owner, George P. Dickson.)

In 1933 at the Tulsa Mid-Continent Kennel Club Show, a dog was entered in the American-Bred Class. This was Philmont Boy, by Sonny Del'Eufer ex Adeline. (Breeder, Waite Phillips. Listed October 22, 1932. Owner, Mrs. Jno K. Curran.) This dog went on to Fourth in Group. According to our club Historian, Dave Spang, this probably was the first Belgian Sheepdog to place in Group.

In the twenties and thirties dog shows ran for three days, and most were held in tents. There were few comfortable accommodations available and many people slept in the tents with their dogs. The shows were small and the exhibitors were like a happy family roughing it. When you think of the shows today with the big vans, air conditioners, comfortable buildings to show in, and all the modern equipment, you want to take your hat off to the hardy souls who blazed the trail in the depression years.

Ch. Fume Noir, C.D., BOB at the 1951 BSCA National Specialty. (Ch. Duke Prince x Comtesse Becu du Barry.) Owners, Rush and Shirley Brown. Handler, Shirley Brown.

Thunderstone's Frosty Night. (Blakey of Pindus x Cleo of Pindus.). Owner, W. H. Robbins.

Ch. Belle Noire Onward Bound, C.D.X., High Scoring Dog, 1983 BSCA National Specialty. Owners, Lance and Teresa Willig.

Ch. Charro of Geier Tal. (Zorro of Geier Tal x Ch. Pandora of Geier Tal.) Owners, Marge and Ed Turnquist.

Ch. Zulvo, C.D., BOB, 1952, 1953, and 1955 BSCA National Specialties. Owner-Handler, Rudy Robinson. Judge, Alva Rosenberg.

The Parent Clubs

In 1925, the first Belgian Sheepdog Club of America was elected to membership in The American Kennel Club. The officers of the club were Calvin Augustin, President; Margaret Phelan, Vice-President; and Edward B. Phelan, Secretary/Treasurer.

In the Westminster Dog Show Catalogs of 1928, 1929, and 1930, the same officers were shown. Many of the Belgians were entered as "Listed."

One interesting trophy was offered during that time by Margaret Phelan. It was the Vice-President's Cup, "for the first dog or bitch winning its registration." Another trophy was offered for the dog or bitch having won the most first prizes (blue ribbons) for the year.

The officers of the club were active in showing dogs. Mr. Augustin is listed as the owner of Ch. Marco out of the Galopin and Netty litter bred by Mr. Domus of Canada, and of Ch. Jet of the same litter. The progeny of Galopin and Netty were dominant in the breeding programs of the exhibitors at that time. Calvin Augustin wrote many interesting articles for dog magazines long before becoming President of the parent club and seemed to have a great knowledge of the breed. He was active in breeding and exhibiting his dogs.

One can only speculate on the reason for the dissolution of the first Belgian Sheepdog Club; only the members know the facts.

On February 16, 1947, the second Belgian Sheepdog Club of America was organized at the Field House in Muncie, Indiana. The following officers were elected: Myron "Ted" Rowland, President; Rush L. Brown, First Vice-President; Mildred Shepard, Second Vice-President; Beatrice Brindel, Secretary/Treasurer; Cecil Lutz, W. B. Vestal, and Arthur Brindel, Board of Directors.

Following the organization of the club, a series of sanctioned matches was held in order to fulfill the requirements for recognition by the AKC. The club also needed to pay to the AKC $330.00, which they did not have at that time. The members paid $25.00 each as dues. Ted and Freda Rowland borrowed $175.00 from the bank to cover the cost of ribbons, trophies, and supplies needed for the sanctioned matches.

The first application to the AKC was denied because the club did not have enough members. There were only

Ch. Judy Jedeux Bingen. Owner, Harold Hansen.

Francois du Chemin des Dames. Owners, Arthur and Beatrice Brindel.

Ch. Olivier Fumee, C.D. (Ch. Fume Noir II x Florimel Signe.) Owners, Rush and Shirley Brown.

Left, Ch. Van Mell's Shenandoah, U.D. (Salute America O'Ebon Will x Ch. Vicci's Concertina.) Owners, Paul and Beth Lachnitt.

Above, Zordoff. (Ubro of the Country House x X'Tania de la Haine.) Owner, Angelo Colombo, Italy.

Left, Ch. Arbor Vista's Dusky Lad and Ch. Arbor Vista's Fredia Noir. Owners, Gene and Joanne Summers.

thirteen members at the time, but the club worked harder and acquired more. As the club grew, the loan from the Rowlands was repaid.

In the minutes of the May 1949 meeting, plans were made to contact the AKC and ask that the club's application be reconsidered. Again, however, because of the loss of members, the club almost folded. Rudy Robinson, Arthur Brindel, Rush Brown, and W. B. Vestal each loaned the club $25.00 until it could get back on its feet again. More new members were added and more sanctioned matches were held. The club applied to the AKC again in December 1949 and at that time was accepted into membership.

In the minutes of a Board of Directors meeting in March 1952, a motion was made and carried that the following charter members be listed in the permanent records of the club: W. B. Vestal, Cecil Lutz, Beatrice Brindel, Arthur Brindel, Rush Brown, Shirley Brown, Rudolf Robinson, Myron Rowland, Freda Rowland, Mildred L. Shepard, Perry Daily, Marguerite Daily, Ed Hauser, and Mrs. Ed Hauser.

As the club began to grow, other names appeared in later records of the minutes. Among these were Norton, Goris, Mertz, Mills, Orrin Stine, John Cowley, and Margaret Coyle. Many others followed.

Ch. Lawry Candide, C.D., BOB, 1962 and 1966 BSCA National Specialties. (Ch. Zulvo, C.D. x Gama des Ardennes du Coitron.) Owner, Gloria L. Davis. Photo by William Gilbert.

Ch. Vicci's Tamarin. (Thunderstone's Frosty Night x Zenabeth of Geier Tal.) Owner, Carole Vander-Meulen. Photo by Morry Twomey.

The charter members imported a number of dogs from some of the best kennels in Europe. The club was small, but with the imports the members had a good genetic pool from which to choose in establishing breeding programs. They bred many very good dogs that had a great influence on the breed at a time when revitalization was necessary. Those of us who came into the club in the fifties benefited from the early members' trials and errors, and remember the dogs and the people who made it all possible. The club grew quite rapidly in the fifties, and club membership has increased every year and now approaches five hundred. To name every person or kennel that has contributed to the success of the club and to Belgian Sheepdogs would be impossible. Belgian Sheepdogs are taking their rightful place in Group placements and Best-in-Show awards. It has been a long, rocky road for this versatile breed of dog that is finally being recognized as one of the most proficient dogs in the Herding Group as well as a companion for people of all ages.

Ch. Fume Noir, C.D., BOB at the 1951 BSCA National Specialty. (Ch. Duke Prince x Comtesse Jeanne Becu du Barry.) Owners, Rush and Shirley Brown.

Ch. Roll In & C Bonita, C.D., BOS, 1961 BSCA National Specialty. (Ch. Quilhot's Jimmie Gene x Ch. Rowland's Vicki de Beaute Noir, C.D.) Breeder-Handler, Freda Rowland.

Pillars of the Breed

The following are only brief sketches of some of the charter members of the BSCA and their dogs, vital participants in the reorganization of the Belgian Sheepdog Club of America, Inc.

W. B. Vestal was a member of the first Belgian Sheepdog Club of America and was a charter member of the reorganized BSCA in 1947. He and his wife bred many fine Belgians and were active in showing their dogs in both conformation shows and obedience classes.

Mrs. Vestal was probably best known for training and showing Ch. Hadji de Flanders, U.D.T., the first Belgian to be granted the two highest titles at that time, Utility Dog and Utility Dog Tracking. Hadji was trained not only for shows but also for the most important job—usefulness in everyday living. Hadji won his tracking title in his ninth year and his championship the next year—quite a feat for a dog at that age. He was trained for Red Cross rescue work and participated in exhibitions to recruit dogs for defense, and entertained wounded G.I.'s in hospitals. Hadji, assisted by Mrs. Vestal, collected subscription pledges for Guide Dogs for the Blind. They were a wonderful combination of a lady and her dog being useful to their fellow man.

Rush and Shirley Brown got their first Belgian, Ch. Fleur Ebon de Beaute Noir, C.D., from Art and Bea Brindel of Muncie, Indiana. The Browns were charter members of the present BSCA. They have maintained a kennel of the highest quality Belgian Sheepdogs for many years. They both were active club members, showing in both conformation and obedience. Their record of achievements in all fields of endeavor is second to none. Their devotion to the breed and to high standards have made their role in the advancement of the breed a very important one.

Most people in the fancy are familiar with Ch. Fume Noir, C.D., or Smokey, as he was called, who was one of their foundation dogs and played an important part in establishing their line.

In 1948, Rush Brown, Arthur Brindel, and E. W. Hauser were appointed by the club to research the history of the breed for a booklet for club members. Mr. Hauser took on the job of researching literature and reference material for facts about the breed. Rush Brown and Mr. Brindel worked back through former breeders and

Duke Prince. (Francois du Chemin des Dames x Star de Flanders.) Owner, Mildred Shepard.

Ch. Roll In Guzzie, C.D., BOB, 1968 BSCA National Specialty. Owners, Myron and Freda Rowland.

77

followed the chain of imports back to Belgium and France. This exhaustive search for facts took the three men eighteen months. They compiled the material, and the booklet was printed. Very few people realize how much effort these dedicated people expended for the club.

Rudy Robinson probably put more resources into importing good strains of Belgian Sheepdogs from Europe than any other breeder of his time. He promoted the breed through advertising in dog magazines, his pamphlets on the breed, and his own newsletter for his customers. Some of his well-known dogs were Sheba III de Beaute Noir, U.D., who appeared in many of his ads; Vicky and Vivette du Mont Sara; Billy von Lerchenberg; and Champions Yedo, Zuzu de L'Infernal, Zita de L'Infernal, Zulvo, Arta du Chemin des Dames, and Gama des Ardennes du Coitron; and an entire litter from the Pirata Nero Kennels in Italy, owned by Angelo Colombo. This litter of five dogs and two bitches was sired by Zordoff, a dog proclaimed "Champion of Italy."

Zordoff was a half-brother of Ch. Zulvo, C.D., Rudy's well-known imported dog and the producer of many champions. Rudy wanted to buy Zordoff but the dog was not for sale for any amount of money. Rudy Robinson and

Etoile of Muncietta. (Duke Prince x Comtesse Jeanne Becu du Barry.) Owner, Mildred Shepard.

Ch. Ginger de Beaute Noir. (Bravo de Beaute Noir, C.D. x Ch. Dianne de Beaute Noir, C.D.) Owner, Mildred Shepard.

Orrin Stine began corresponding with Mr. Colombo in an attempt to secure a couple of fine specimens sired by Zordoff. Mr. Colombo was so conscientious in his desire to supply the right specimens that he wrote to Robinson and Stine a letter which said, "In order to be sure that you get the best specimens, I am going to ship you the entire litter." This was a bit more than they had bargained for, but the deal was made and the twelve-week-old litter was shipped. In that litter were two Belgians with which most people are familiar: Ch. Liza del Pirata Nero, C.D. (who became the Queen Mother of the Geier Tal Kennels in Oklahoma, owned by the Turnquists), and Ch. Tazir II del Pirata Nero, owned by Ted and Freda Rowland of Roll In Kennels.

Mr. Colombo bought up the best specimens of the now disbanded Mont Sara Kennels of Belgium, with the aim of preserving the fast-disappearing small ear. The small correct ears were quite evident in his dogs and in the litter that he sent Rudy Robinson.

Mr. Colombo was presented with a full-size bronze replica of a Belgian Sheepdog for his integrity in breeding and for his dedication to the breed.

Grandfond Amazone Noire. Owner, Kaye Hall.

In 1957, the Rowlands formed a partnership with Sam and Freda Chandler, and the kennel name became Roll In & C. The merger of the two kennels produced many fine Belgians which placed in Groups and were Best of Breed at the National Specialty Shows.

Freda Rowland was a familiar sight in the show ring. She was a remarkable person. She was familiar with all the Belgians at that time and could remember the name of the breeder of any Belgian and recite the dog's pedigree from memory. We called her the walking encyclopedia of the breed. She never was too busy to answer letters and give advice and encouragement to beginners in the breed. The latchstring was always out at the Rowlands. Freda was an excellent cook and nothing pleased her more than having old friends around the table to dine and to discuss dogs.

Freda Rowland died in 1970 at a National Specialty, and since 1971 a Freda Rowland Memorial Trophy, in the form of a large silver bowl, has been given by the BSCA in her memory. Each year this bowl graces the trophy table at the National Specialty, and a smaller replica is given the BOB winner. The name of the winning dog is engraved on the memorial trophy.

Barry de Jean. Owner, Mildred Shepard.

With the acquisition by Rudy Robinson of the Pirata Nero line, Groenendaels from Switzerland, Belgium, Italy, and France were placed under one kennel roof. Each specimen represented Europe's best bloodlines, with characteristics that American breeders wanted to introduce into their strains. One interesting observation made to Rudy Robinson by a foreign breeder who had observed American Belgians was, "Push down those ears until the chest drops another inch."

Ted and Freda Rowland of Roll In Kennels purchased their first Belgian, Ch. Vicki de Beaute Noir, from Art and Bea Brindel in 1945. This beginning led to over thirty years of breeding and training Belgian Sheepdogs. Their many champions and fine breeding stock were well known by the Belgian fancy. They were charter members of the present parent club and worked in all club activities to help organize the club and promote the breed. In 1955, they acquired Ch. Tazir del Pirata Nero from Rudy Robinson. "Ricky," as he was called, passed on squareness, small ears, and beautiful straight coats to his progeny, traits which were needed at that time. He was a great asset to Roll In Kennels.

Roll In Kennels are gone now, but Roll In and Roll In & C's dogs' names still appear on pedigrees all over the country.

Arthur and Beatrice Brindel became interested in Belgian Sheepdogs in 1942. Their stock came from a pair of Belgians from the kennels of Mrs. Cecil Lutz. The first Belgian Sheepdog to become an American champion after World War II was a bitch bred by the Brindels, Ch. Dianne de Beaute Noir, C.D.X. Many more champions came from the Black Beauty Kennels. Ch. Dianne de Beaute Noir, C.D.X., is credited with being the first bitch to acquire the C.D.X. title.

Beatrice Brindel became Secretary/Treasurer of the reorganized BSCA in 1947 and remained in that position for several years. The Brindels were very active exhibitors and served in many capacities in the reorganized club. Many of the charter members give them credit for being an important force in holding the club together when it was trying to gain recognition from the AKC.

When the Brindels gave up their kennels in Muncie, Indiana, and moved to Florida, Mr. Brindel became active

Ch. Dulci Candide, left, and Ch. Barbi Candide, with Rudy Robinson.

Ch. Tazir III del Pirata Nero. (Zordoff x Sjla del Pirata Nero.) Owners, Myron and Freda Rowland.

in teaching obedience classes. They took their two favorite dogs with them, Sheba II de Belique and Francois de Chemin des Dames, or "Bing." Bing was in the pedigrees of many of the best Belgians in America at that time. The Brindels were not able to finish his championship because of his being hit by a car, which left him lame. He was an excellent guard dog at their home. Mr. Brindel told an amusing story about a stranger approaching their house and meeting the big black dog blocking the entrance. The man tried to kick him out of the way. Bing caught his foot and set him down hard, then barked until Mr. Brindel told him it was all right.

The Brindels did not resume their breeding of Belgians after moving to Florida, but remained great boosters of the breed.

Mildred Shepard got her first Belgian Sheepdog from the Brindels in the forties. She was a charter member of the reorganized BSCA and remained active in the club until recently. Many fine dogs came from her Shady Lawn Kennels. Mildred was Second Vice-President of the first

Wildfire at Coaltree, C.D., and Ch. Laralee's Personality, C.D.X., A.D., Sch-H I. Owner, Pat Crabtree.

active breeder and exhibitor. Like those of some of the other old breeders, his kennel records and pictures have been lost.

All the members from the early days contributed their efforts toward bringing the breed back into recognition when interest waned after the demise of the first BSCA. It was the opinion of many of the older breeders that Belgians were used in police work to such an extent at that time that people began to associate them more with that type of work and did not trust them as family dogs. It took many years to dispel this image.

In 1950 Belgian Sheepdogs started their upward swing in Group placements. Throughout the ensuing years they have continued their success in Group and Best in Show awards. The breed has come a long way since the first Belgian came to a strange new country, unknown and unheralded, with only his beauty to recommend him. He still had to prove his utilitarian possibilities. His courage and good qualities, promoted by staunch supporters, proved that the pioneer Belgians were an asset to their adopted country. No longer strangers, Belgians have taken their rightful place in society.

Ch. Zulvo, C.D., BOB, 1952, 1953, and 1955 BSCA National Specialties. Owner, Rudy Robinson.

Board of Directors in 1947. Several sanctioned matches were held at the Shepard farm in Delphi, Indiana.

A few of her dogs were Ch. Ginger de Beaute Noir, Duke Prince, Ch. Black Bond, Etoile of Muncietta, and Contessa Becu du Barry.

Mr. and Mrs. Cecil Lutz lived in Pennsylvania. In 1945, Mrs. Lutz imported several Belgian Sheepdogs, and through her efforts the Arthur Brindels and Myron Rowlands became interested in the breed. The Brindels got their Francois du Chemin des Dames and Sheba II de Belique from the Lutzes.

Mr. Lutz was a member of the first Board of Directors in 1947. The Lutzes were active breeders but their records have been lost over the years.

Mr. A. F. Goris, of Long Island, New York, imported three dogs after World War I. He went to Europe and selected three more after World War II. Two of the dogs he imported were Moto du Mont Sara, and Minora. Mr. Goris's kennel name was Beldome.

Mr. Goris was not a charter member, but he was an

Left to right: Am. and Mex. Ch. Brown's Jeamill of Hamor, C.D.; Ch. Dione's Dynamite Jani; and Ch. Solange Ace of Spades. Photo by Rich Bergman.

Mr. Leo Light, owner, with five Belgians at Sled Dog Derby, Winnepeg Beach, Manitoba, Canada. The lead dog is Black Diamond of Ganymede. Mattern Photo.

Kennels—Past and Present

The following are kennels that made their mark in the history of the breed but are no longer active.

Kennel Name	Owner(s)	Location
Arbor Vista's	Alfred Schneider	
Bar-K	Robert Krohn	New Mexico
Beldome	August Goris	New York
Beltrod	Dorothy Andrews	Massachusetts
Candide	Rudolph Robinson	Illinois
De Beaute Belge	J. Dolphe Mills	Indiana
De Beaute Noir	The Brindels	Indiana
Del Rio Carmells	The Vestals	Arizona
Roll In	M. E. Rowland	Indiana
Roll In & C	Sam Chandler	Indiana
Nether-Lair	John Cowley	Massachusetts
Quilhot's	Helen Quilhot	Indiana
Shady Lawn	Mildred Shepard	Indiana

Ryan Wagoner and pals go jogging. Owners, Shane and Kathay Wagoner, Blue Lake Belgians.

Present-Day Kennels

The following is a list of kennel names of members of the Belgian Sheepdog Club of America, Inc. It is not a complete list, but includes only those made available to the author.

Kennel Name	Owner(s)	Location
AH's	Donna Albro & Lois Hasty	Fort Worth, Texas
Aleika	Stephanie Price	Melbourne, Florida
Aljanwood	Alice Woodward	Concord, California
Avatar	Barbara Swisher	Oak Park, Illinois
A-Yacht's	James Ayotte	Grand Rapids, Michigan
A-Z Belgians	Anna Zolan	Baytown, Texas
Barb-Eck's	Barbara Eklund	Albuquerque, New Mexico
Beaux	Mary Bowie	Winterport, Maine
Belfry	Judith Bell	Weatherford, Texas
Belle Noire	Carolyn Hackney	Bartlesville, Oklahoma
Belmont	Hildegard Buschman	Mountain Lake, New Jersey
Berthier	Drs. Robert & Nancy Bethea	Lubbock, Texas
Bingen	Mary K. Dillaway	Plymouth, Massachusetts
Blackfire	Patricia Peters	Crest Hill, Illinois
Blue Lake	Shane & Kathay Wagoner	Lake Tahoe, California
Bo-Mar	Marjorie De Mille	Las Vegas, Nevada
Brajac	Kathy Smith	Unity, Oregon
Brandon Bluff	Pat Savard	Morgan Hill, California
Breines	Ira Breine	Lebanon, New Jersey
Bren-Joe	Joel & Brenda Levine	Freehold, New Jersey
Britwald	Barbara Salberg	Wingdale, New York
Calia-Cavalier	Carole and Amelia Eklund	Atascadero, California
Carboncrest	Dr. Carol Stein	Johnstown, Ohio
Carlian	Carol Thompson	Dedham, Massachusetts
Carrillon	Carol Madden	Omaha, Nebraska
C'est Si Bon	Gloria Davis	Baltimore, Maryland
Charfire	Grover and Elaine Haven	Orange, California
Char Mar	Charlene Muscuch	Watchung, New Jersey
Chasseur	Gail Hunter	Fresno, California
Chenior	Judith Smith	Royal Oak, Michigan
Chieho	Elaine Jaye	Lansing, Michigan
Claire de Lune	Claire Trethewey	APO, New York
Coalfire	Chet and Ronna Kowal	Port Orchard, Washington
Coaltree	Patricia Crabtree	Dallas, Texas

Left, Ch. Coaltree's Texas Spitfire, C.D., A.D.; center, Devon Wheeler; right, Ch. Coaltree Calypso at Spitfire.

Ike V. Siegestor, C.D.X., T.D. Owner, Mary Courter.

Am. and Can. Ch. Mi-Sha-Ook's Lunar Shade. (Ch. Star de la Baraque de Planches x Ch. A-Yacht's Conita.) Owner-Handler, Kathleen Mahaffey. Judge, Mr. Felton. Photo by John Ashbey.

Ch. Dexter Noquar Bingen. (Ch. Charro of Geier Tal x Ch. Noel Mitres Bingen, C.D.) Breeder-Owner-Handler, Mary Dillaway (Bingen Kennels). Photo by William Gilbert.

Am. and Mex. Ch. Brown's Jeamill of Hamor, C.D., BOB, 1975 BSCA National Specialty. (Salute America O'Ebon Will, U.D. x Ch. Lacy Lady of Black Dawn, C.D.) Owners, Millard and Jeani Brown (Jeamill's Kennels).

Kennel Name	**Owner(s)**	**Location**
Courter's	Mary Courter	Grantsburg, Illinois
Crocs-Blanc's	Daniele Daugherty	Highland, Michigan
Crosswinds	Kathleen Mahaffey	Reinhold, Pennsylvania
Czequet Belgians	Al and Cindy Czech	Loomis, California
Dan-Lin	Linda Gaymon	Camden, Ohio
De Avila	Ruth Avila	Granite Falls, Washington
De Berger	June Maul	White House Station, New Jersey
Deemar	Denise Ondersma	Delton, Michigan
De Jez Lancaster	Cecil Lancaster	Kittery, Maine

Ch. Noire Aimee's Midnight Magic, BOB, 1982 BSCA National Specialty. Owner, Kathy Bober (Rhiannon Kennels).

Van Mell's Trouble in Paradise. (Ch. Donovan of High Mount x Ch. Van Mell's Hells O'Ebon Will.) Owners, Carole Vander-Meulen (Van Mell's Kennels) and Frank Shreve. Judge, J. N. Kay.

Ch. High-Mount's Pride of Quivala, BOB, 1977 BSCA National Specialty. (Ch. Quivala de la Baraque de Planches x Ch. High-Mount's Charmin. Owner, Helena Brown (High-Mount Kennels). Judge, Louis Harris. Photo by John Ashbey.

Kennel Name	Owner(s)	Location
Del'Affair	Deanna Kruglick	Winnetka, Illinois
De La Fusee	Sharon Lafuse	Houston, Texas
Delting	Marie Martin	Odessa, Texas
Dione	Christlin Hyde	La Canada, California
Dream On	Marcia Bailey	Wever, Ohio
Eaglevale	Jerrilyn Wilson	Quartz Hill, California
E'bon Will	Terry Goshen	Lafayette, Colorado
Endymion	Marc Hessel	Centre Hall, Pennsylvania
Eyass	Sunny Stock	Drexel, Missouri
Fairwinds	Lou Ann Walker	Summerville, South Carolina
Fashion Walk	Donald Goodman	Pittsburg, California
Fre-Cin	Frederick Pisani	N. Canton, Ohio
Frenchtown	Janie Carter	St. Charles, Missouri
Fume de Fleur	Shirley Brown	Noblesville, Indiana
Ganymede	Sheila Rentschler	Woodinville, Washington
Geier Tal	Marge Turnquist	Tulsa, Oklahoma
Geka	Dottie Lee	Lancaster, Texas
Go-Lynn	Gordon Peterson	Elk River, Minnesota
Greenfields	Ellen K. Haro	Davis, California
Haljean	Harold & Jean Hansen	Arlington, Massachusetts
Hallmark	Judi DeRosa	Yuba City, California
Harper's Belgians	Ann Harper	Dallas, Texas
Heidelweiss	Herbert Stuber	Bend, Oregon
Heritage	Carol Ann Cucinotta	Cincinnati, Ohio
High-Mount	Helena Brown	Patterson, New York
Hollandia's	Joan McCann	Centerport, New York
Incha-Alla	Heike Wehrle	S. Elgin, Illinois
Iselheim Belgians	Janet Reisig	Pelleston, Michigan
Isengard	Lorra Acord	Concord, California
Jacamar	Marilyn Russel	Bangor, Maine
Jeamill	Millard & Jeani Brown	Burbank, California
Johnsondale	Pat Johnson	S. Charleston, Ohio
Jostin	Kristin Fleugel	Anoka, Minnesota
Keldestra	William & Carolyn Dotson	Davis, California
Lancets	Dr. Donald Wald	San Francisco, California
Lan-Krest	Walter Schleicher	New York

Ch. Laralee's Cricket de Berthier. Owner-Handler, Dr. Nancy Bethea (Berthier Kennels.) Judge, Glenn Sommers. Photo by Morry Twomey.

Ch. C'est Si Bon Astarte Huce. Owner, Gloria L. Davis (C'est Si Bon Kennels).

Kennel Name	Owner(s)	Location
Laralee's	Laura Patton	Dallas, Texas
Laurel	Wanda Martin	Reinhold, Pennsylvania
L'Ecossais	Shirley Howard	W. Chicago, Illinois
Le Grand Fond	Kaye Hall	Napa, California
Lightfoot	Dawn Manson	Brooklyn, New York
Liket	Beth Lachnitt	Duncanville, Texas
Lorahame	Freya Robison	Dallas, Texas
Lorgen	Roger & Maxine Ellis	Belle Mead, New Jersey
Lorlyndel Belgians	David and Ruth Fullaway	Maui, Hawaii
Loup Noir	Mary Linda Adams	Oxford, Massachusetts
Maree	Russell Randall	Burbank, California
Mar-Rod	Marlene Freyburger	Tucson, Arizona
Mawrmyth	Marcy Spalding	Houston, Texas
Methow Belgians	Jan Stratton	Chehalis, Washington
Midnight Acres	Melodee Tragnitz	Crete, Illinois
Mi-Sha-Ook	Lawrence Stanbridge	Canada
Mons	Madeline Pragnell	Victor, Montana
Night Life	Mary Ann Weber	Franklin Park, Illinois
Noire Aimee	Elinore Rogers	Pleasant Mt., Pennsylvania
Noir-Royale	Susan Vaccarelli	Somerville, New Jersey
Odyssey	Rita Hill	Decatur, Georgia
One More Belgians	Linda Gayman	Gratis, Ohio
Pentara	John Pendell	Phoenix, Arizona
Peppertom	Pamela Thomsen	Chula Vista, California
Pine Valley	T. E. Young	Maben, Mississippi
Raular	Morton Rau	Haymarket, Virginia
Ravenwood	Elinor McDonald	Colt's Neck, New Jersey
Rhiannon	Kathleen Bober	Camillus, New York
Rolin Ridge	Linda McCarty	Richmond, Virginia
Runes	Pat Woicek	Park Forest, Illinois
Sandarac	Sue Arn	Simi Valley, California
Sandevel	Sandra King	Taylor Ridge, Illinois

Ch. Banjoette O'Ebon Will, U.D., BOS, 1973 BSCA National Specialty. (Ch. A-Yacht's Banjo Boy x Ch. Dark Angel of Ebon Tide, U.D.) Owner, Terry Hendricks.

Ch. Zachariah Coburg of Van Mell, C.D.X., BOB, 1976 BSCA National Specialty. (Ch. Witch Doctor's Majesty x Ch. Vicci's Concertina.) Owners, John and Darlene Eaton (The House of Coburg Kennels).

Kennel Name	Owner(s)	Location
Sanlyn	Herbert Springsteen	Nanuet, New York
Sans	Norman Benfer	Norco, California
Sans Branco	Terri Ann Votava	Sylvan Lake, Michigan
Sherborne	Jill Sherer	Jay, Oklahoma
Shez-Les-Bels	Kathleen Herman	Crystal Lake, Illinois
Shardix	Rodney Adams	Gilbert, Arizona
Shimka	Lynn Van Duyne	Hamburg, Pennsylvania
Siegestor	Kurt Marti	Claremont, California
Skywalker	John Danielson	Watertown, Wisconsin
Sky Watchers	Kathy Graham	Reno, Nevada
Solange	Joel Backer	Los Altos, California
Solamarcs	Mary Jane Buckman	Bethel, Pennsylvania
Spirit	Rasa Moser	Burbank, Illinois
Spitfire	Anita Meeks Wheeler	Dallas, Texas
Star Castle	Sue Whited	Richmond, Indiana
Starwood	Pam Rathkamp	Otego, New York
Sundown	Mike Fine	Mantua, Ohio
Takavor	Marsha Merjanian	Deephaven, Minnesota
Tars	Eloise Robinson	Shreveport, Louisiana
The House of Coburg	John & Darlene Eaton	San Antonio, Texas
Thunderstone	Laura Gray	Gastonia, North Carolina
Toleda	Cleda Copeland	Warrenton, Virginia
Torbrook	Sylvia Banks	Canada
Touraline	Janet Constable	Morristown, Tennessee
Valley View	Martha Lange	Council Bluff, Iowa
Val Valle's	Artice Mainville	Dimendale, Michigan
Van Mell's	Carole Vander-Meulen	Crandall, Texas
Vicon	Celeste Weeks	Virginia Beach, Virginia
Voudoun's	Margery Riddle	Berkeley, California
Webelo	Vicki Bremer	Maple Grove, Minnesota
Wildland	Linda Elligott	Newfield, New Jersey
Winterwood	Sue Shuetz	Verona, Wisconsin
Witchhollow	Patricia Krueger	Nashua, New Hampshire
Wolfstar	Elaine Kelley	Eatontown, New Jersey
Xanth Belgians	Leslie Campbell	Lubbock, Texas

Ch. Belle Noire Torreon. (Ch. Charro of Geier Tal x Ch. Van Mell's Dynasty, C.D.) Owners, Marge and Ed Turnquist (Geier Tal Kennels).

Ch. Lorahame's Slippery Roc, C.D. (Ch. Laralee's Rebel Roc O'Lorahame, C.D.X., Sch-H I x Ch. Lorahame Roc N'Rally, C.D.) Owners, Freya Robison (Lorahame Kennels) and Sue Sivess.

Genetics

Genetics, the science of heredity, deals with the processes by which physical and mental traits of parents are transmitted to offspring. For centuries, man has been trying to solve these puzzles, but only in the last two hundred years has significant progress been made.

During the eighteenth century, Kolreuter, a German scientist, made revolutionary discoveries concerning plant sexuality and hybridization but was unable to explain just how hereditary processes worked. In the middle of the nineteenth century, Gregor Johann Mendel, an Augustinian monk, experimented with the ordinary garden pea and made other discoveries of major significance. He found that an inherited characteristic was inherited as a complete unit, and that certain characteristics predominated over others. Next, he observed that the hereditary characteristics of each parent are contained in each offspring, even when they are not visible, and that "hidden" characteristics can be transferred without change in their nature to the grandchildren, or even later generations. Finally, he concluded that although heredity contains an element of uncertainty, some things are predictable on the basis of well-defined mathematical laws.

Unfortunately, Mendel's published paper went unheeded, and when he died in 1884 he was still virtually unknown to the scientific world. But other researchers were making discoveries, too. In 1900, three different scientists reported to learned societies that much of their research in hereditary principles had been proved years before by Gregor Mendel and that findings matched perfectly.

Thus, hereditary traits were proved to be transmitted through the chromosomes found in pairs in every living being, one of each pair contributed by the mother, the other by the father. Within each chromosome have been found hundreds of smaller structures, or genes, which are the actual determinants of hereditary characteristics. Some genes are dominant and will be seen in the offspring. Others are recessive and will not be outwardly apparent, yet can be passed on to the offspring to combine with a similar recessive gene of the other parent and thus be seen. Or they may be passed on to the offspring, not be outwardly apparent, but be passed on again to become apparent in a later generation.

Once the genetic theory of inheritance became widely known, scientists began drawing a well-defined line between inheritance and environment. More recent studies show some overlapping of these influences and indicate a combination of the two may be responsible for certain characteristics. For instance, studies have proved that extreme cold increases the amount of black pigment in the skin and hair of the "Himalayan" rabbit, although it has little or no effect on the white or colored rabbit. Current research also indicates that even though characteristics are determined by the genes, some environmental stress occurring at a particular period of pregnancy might cause physical change in the embryo.

Long before breeders had any knowledge of genetics, they practiced one of its most important principles—selective breeding. Experience quickly showed that "like begets like," and by breeding like with like and discarding unlike offspring, the various individual breeds were developed to the point where variations were relatively few. Selective breeding is based on the idea of maintaining the quality of a breed at the highest possible level, while improving whatever defects are prevalent. It requires that only the top dogs in a litter be kept for later breeding, and that inferior specimens be ruthlessly eliminated.

In planning any breeding program, the first requisite is a definite goal—that is, to have clearly in mind a definite picture of the type of dog you wish eventually to produce. To attempt to breed perfection is to approach the problem unrealistically. But if you don't breed for improvement, it is preferable that you not breed at all.

As a first step, you should select a bitch that exemplifies as many of the desired characteristics as possible and mate her with a dog that also has as many of the desired characteristics as possible. If you start with mediocre pets, you will produce mediocre pet puppies. If you decided to start with more than one bitch, all should closely approach the type you desire, since you will then stand a better chance of producing uniformly good puppies from all. Breeders often start with a single bitch and keep the best bitches in every succeeding generation.

Experienced breeders look for "prepotency" in breeding stock—that is, the ability of a dog or bitch to transmit traits to most or all of its offspring. While the term is usually used to describe the transmission of good qualities, a dog may also be prepotent in transmitting faults. To be prepotent in a practical sense, a dog must possess many characteristics controlled by dominant genes. If desired characteristics are recessive, they will be apparent in the offspring only if carried by both sire and dam. Prepotent dogs and bitches usually come from a line of prepotent ancestors, but the mere fact that a dog has exceptional ancestors will not necessarily mean that he himself will produce exceptional offspring.

A single dog may sire a tremendous number of puppies, whereas a bitch can produce only a comparatively few litters during her lifetime. Thus, a sire's influence may be very widespread as compared to that of a bitch. But in evaluating a particular litter, it must be remembered that the bitch has had as much influence as has had the dog.

Inbreeding, line-breeding, outcrossing, or a combination of the three are the methods commonly used in selective breeding.

Left, Ch. Gama des Ardennes du Coitron. Owner, Gloria L. Davis. Photo by Charles Smith.

Above, Ch. Quivala de la Baraque de Planches. (Kilt De Lamara x Nolette de la Baraque de Planches.) Owner, Sheila Rentschler.

Left, Ch. Danny Boy of Ganymede. (Ch. Quivala de la Baraque de Planches x Ch. High-Mount's Charmin.) Owner, Lloyd Rentschler.

Inbreeding is the mating together of closely related animals, such as father-daughter, mother-son, or brother-sister. Although some breeders insist such breeding will lead to the production of defective individuals, it is through rigid inbreeding that all breeds of dogs have been established. Controlled tests have shown that any harmful effects appear within the first five or ten generations, and that if rigid selection is exercised from the beginning, a vigorous inbred strain will be built up.

Line-breeding is also the mating together of individuals related by family lines. However, matings are made not so much on the basis of the dog's and bitch's relationship to each other, but instead, on the basis of their relationship to a highly admired ancestor, with a view to perpetuating that ancestor's qualities. Line-breeding constitutes a long-range program and cannot be accomplished in a single generation.

Outcrossing is the breeding together of two dogs that are unrelated in family lines. Actually, since breeds have been developed through the mating of close relatives, all dogs within any given breed are related to some extent. There are few breedings that are true outcrosses, but if there is no common ancestor within five generations, a mating is usually considered an outcross.

Experienced breeders sometimes outcross for one generation in order to eliminate a particular fault, then go back to inbreeding or line-breeding. Neither the good effects nor the bad effects of outcrossing can be truly evaluated in a single mating, for undesirable recessive traits may be introduced into a strain, yet not show up for several generations. Outcrossing is better left to experienced breeders, for continual outcrossing results in a wide variation in type and great uncertainty as to the results that may be expected.

Two serious defects that are believed heritable—subluxation and orchidism—should be zealously guarded against, and afflicted dogs and their offspring should be eliminated from breeding programs. Subluxation is a condition of the hip joint where the bone of the socket is eroded and the head of the thigh bone is also worn away, causing lameness which becomes progressively more serious until the dog is unable to walk. Orchidism is the failure of one or both testicles to develop and descend properly. When one testicle is involved, the term "monorchid" is used. When both are involved, "cryptorchid" is used. A cryptorchid is almost always sterile, whereas a monorchid is usually fertile. There is evidence that orchidism "runs in families" and that a monorchid transmits the tendency through bitch and male puppies alike.

Through the years, many misconceptions concerning heredity have been perpetuated. Perhaps the one most widely perpetuated is the idea evolved hundreds of years ago that somehow characteristics were passed on through

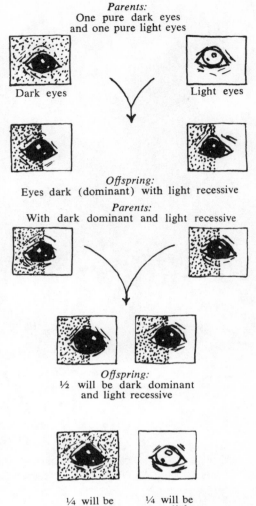

Parents:
One pure dark eyes and one pure light eyes

Dark eyes   Light eyes

Offspring:
Eyes dark (dominant) with light recessive

Parents:
With dark dominant and light recessive

Offspring:
½ will be dark dominant and light recessive

¼ will be   ¼ will be
pure dark   pure light

The above is a schematic representation of the Mendelian law as it applies to the inheritance of eye color. The law applies in the same way to the inheritance of other physical characteristics.

the mixing of the blood of the parents. We still use terminology evolved from that theory when we speak of bloodlines, or describe individuals as full-blooded, despite the fact that the theory was disproved more than a century ago.

Also inaccurate and misleading is any statement that a definite fraction or proportion of an animal's inherited characteristics can be positively attributed to a particular ancestor. Individuals lacking knowledge of genetics sometimes declare that an individual receives half his inherited characteristics from each parent, a quarter from each grandparent, an eighth from each great-grandparent, etc. Thousands of volumes of scientific findings have been published, but no simple way has been found to determine positively which characteristics have been inherited from which ancestors, for the science of heredity is infinitely complex.

Ch. Mawrmyth Cyrena and Am. and Can. Ch. Mi-Sha-Ook's Wonita. Owner, Marcella Spalding (Mawrmyth Kennels).

Ch. A-Yacht's Ben, BOB, 1979 and 1980 BSCA National Specialties. Owner, Heike Wehrle (Incha-Alla Kennels).

Belle Noire Laxson du Jet. (Ch. Jaye's Von Jet x Ch. Belle Noir Granada.) Owner, Kaye Hall (Le Grand Fond Kennels).

Ch. Highmount Demon of Ganymede (Ch. Quivala de la Baraque de Planches x Ch. High-Mount's Charmin.) Owner, Sheila Rentschler (Ganymede Kennels).

Breeding and Whelping

The breeding life of a bitch begins when she comes into season the first time at the age of eight to ten months. Thereafter, she will come in season at roughly six-month intervals. Her maximum fertility builds up from puberty to full maturity and then declines until a state of total sterility is reached in old age. Just when this occurs is hard to determine, for the fact that an older bitch shows signs of being in season doesn't necessarily mean she is still capable of reproducing.

The length of the season varies from eighteen to twenty-one days. The first indication is a pronounced swelling of the vulva with coincidental bleeding (called "showing color") for about the first seven to nine days. The discharge gradually turns to a creamy color, and it is during this phase (estrus), from about the tenth to fifteenth days, that the bitch is ovulating and is receptive to the male. The ripe, unfertilized ova survive for about seventy-two hours. If fertilization doesn't occur, the ova die and are discharged the next time the bitch comes in season. If fertilization does take place, each ovum attaches itself to the walls of the uterus, a membrane forms to seal it off, and a foetus develops from it.

Following the estrus phase, the bitch is still in season until about the twenty-first day and will continue to be attractive to males, although she will usually fight them off as she did the first few days. Nevertheless, to avoid accidental mating, the bitch must be confined for the entire period. Virtual imprisonment is necessary, for male dogs display uncanny abilities in their efforts to reach a bitch in season.

The odor that attracts the males is present in the bitch's urine, so it is advisable to take her a good distance from the house before permitting her to relieve herself. To eliminate problems completely, your veterinarian can prescribe a preparation that will disguise the odor but will not interfere with breeding when the time is right. Many fanciers use such preparations when exhibiting a bitch and find that nearby males show no interest whatsoever. But it is not advisable to permit a bitch to run loose when she has been given a product of this type, for during estrus she will seek the company of male dogs and an accidental mating may occur.

A potential brood bitch, regardless of breed, should have good bone, ample breadth and depth of ribbing, and adequate room in the pelvic region. Unless a bitch is physically mature—well beyond the puppy stage when she has her first season—breeding should be delayed until her second or a later season. Furthermore, even though it is possible for a bitch to conceive twice a year, she should not be bred oftener than once a year. A bitch that is bred too often will age prematurely and her puppies are likely to lack vigor.

Two or three months before a bitch is to be mated, her physical condition should be considered carefully. If she is too thin, provide a rich, balanced diet plus the regular exercise needed to develop strong, supple muscles. Daily exercise on the leash is as necessary for the too-thin bitch as for the too-fat one, although the latter will need more exercise and at a brisker pace, as well as a reduction of food, if she is to be brought to optimum condition. A prospective brood bitch must have had permanent distemper shots as well as rabies vaccination. And a month before her season is due, a veterinarian should examine a stool specimen for worms. If there is evidence of infestation, the bitch should be wormed.

A dog may be used at stud from the time he reaches physical maturity, well on into old age. The first time your bitch is bred, it is well to use a stud that has already proven his ability by having sired other litters. The fact that a neighbor's dog is readily available should not influence your choice, for to produce the best puppies, you must select the stud most suitable from a genetic standpoint.

If the stud you prefer is not going to be available at the time your bitch is to be in season, you may wish to consult your veterinarian concerning medications available for inhibiting the onset of the season. With such preparations, the bitch's season can be delayed indefinitely.

Usually the first service will be successful. However, if it isn't, in most cases an additional service is given free, provided the stud dog is still in the possession of the same owner. If the bitch misses, it may be because her cycle varies widely from normal. Through microscopic examination, a veterinarian can determine exactly when the bitch is entering the estrus phase and thus is likely to conceive.

The owner of the stud should give you a stud-service certificate, providing a four-generation pedigree for the sire and showing the date of the mating. The litter registration application is completed only after the puppies are whelped, but it, too, must be signed by the owner of the stud as well as the owner of the bitch. Registration forms may be secured by writing The American Kennel Club.

In normal pregnancy there is usually visible enlargement of the abdomen by the end of the fifth week. By palpation (feeling with the fingers) a veterinarian may be able to distinguish developing puppies as early as three weeks after mating, but it is unwise for a novice to poke and prod, and try to detect the presence of unborn puppies.

The gestation period normally lasts nine weeks, although it may vary from sixty-one to sixty-five days. If it goes beyond sixty-five days from the date of mating, a veterinarian should be consulted.

During the first four or five weeks, the bitch should be permitted her normal amount of activity. As she becomes

Whelping box. Detail shows proper side-wall construction which helps keep small puppies confined and provides sheltered nook to prevent crushing or smothering.

heavier, she should be walked on the leash, but strenuous running and jumping should be avoided. Her diet should be well balanced (see chapter on nutrition), and if she should become constipated, small amounts of mineral oil may be added to her food.

A whelping box should be secured about two weeks before the puppies are due, and the bitch should start then to use it as her bed so she will be accustomed to it by the time puppies arrive. Preferably, the box should be square, with each side long enough so that the bitch can stretch out full length and have several inches to spare at either end. The bottom should be padded with an old cotton rug or other material that is easily laundered. Edges of the padding should be tacked to the floor of the box so the puppies will not get caught in it and smother. Once it is obvious labor is about to begin, the padding should be covered with several layers of spread-out newspapers. Then, as papers become soiled, the top layer can be pulled off, leaving the area clean.

Forty-eight to seventy-two hours before the litter is to be whelped, a definite change in the shape of the abdomen will be noted. Instead of looking barrel-shaped, the abdomen will sag pendulously. Breasts usually redden and become enlarged, and milk may be present a day or two before the puppies are whelped. As the time becomes imminent, the bitch will probably scratch and root at her bedding in an effort to make a nest, and will refuse food and ask to be let out every few minutes. But the surest sign is a drop in temperature of two or three degrees about twelve hours before labor begins.

The bitch's abdomen and flanks will contract sharply when labor actually starts, and for a few minutes she will attempt to expel a puppy, then rest for a while and try again. Someone should stay with the bitch the entire time whelping is taking place, and if she appears to be having unusual difficulties, a veterinarian should be called.

Puppies are usually born head first, though some may be born feet first and no difficulty encountered. Each puppy is enclosed in a separate membranous sac that the bitch will remove with her teeth. She will sever the umbilical cord, which will be attached to the soft, spongy afterbirth that is expelled right after the puppy emerges. Usually the bitch eats the afterbirth, so it is necessary to watch and make sure one is expelled for each puppy whelped. If afterbirth is retained, the bitch may develop peritonitis and die.

The dam will lick and nuzzle each newborn puppy until it is warm and dry and ready to nurse. If puppies arrive so close together that she can't take care of them, you can help her by rubbing the puppies dry with a soft cloth. If several have been whelped but the bitch continues to be in labor, all but one should be removed and placed in a small box lined with clean towels and warmed to about seventy degrees. The bitch will be calmer if one puppy is left with her at all times.

Whelping sometimes continues as long as twenty-four hours for a very large litter, but a litter of two or three puppies may be whelped in an hour. When the bitch settles down, curls around the puppies and nuzzles them to her, it usually indicates that all have been whelped.

The bitch should be taken away for a few minutes while you clean the box and arrange clean padding. If her coat is soiled, sponge it clean before she returns to the puppies. Once she is back in the box, offer her a bowl of warm beef broth and a pan of cool water, placing both where she will not have to get up in order to reach them. As soon as she indicates interest in food, give her a generous bowl of chopped meat to which codliver oil and dicalcium phosphate have been added.

If inadequate amounts of calcium are provided during the period the puppies are nursing, eclampsia may develop. Symptoms are violent trembling, rapid rise in temperature, and rigidity of muscles. Veterinary assistance must be secured immediately, for death may result in a very short time. Treatment consists of massive doses of calcium gluconate administered intravenously, after which symptoms subside in a miraculously short time.

For weak or very small puppies, supplemental feeding is often recommended. Any one of three different methods may be used: tube-feeding (with a catheter attached to a syringe), using an eyedropper (this method requires great care in order to avoid getting formula in the lungs), or using a tiny bottle (the "pet nurser" available at most pet supply stores). The commercially prepared puppy formulas are most convenient and are readily obtainable from a veterinarian, who can also tell you which method of administering the formula is most practical in your particular case. It is important to remember that equipment must be kept scrupulously clean. It can be sterilized by boiling, or it may be soaked in a Clorox solution, then washed carefully and dried between feedings.

All puppies are born blind and their eyes open when they are ten to fourteen days old. At first the eyes have a bluish cast and appear weak, and the puppies must be protected from strong light until at least ten days after the eyes open.

To ensure proper emotional development, young dogs should be shielded from loud noises and rough handling. Being lifted by the front legs is painful and may result in permanent injury to the shoulders. So when lifting a puppy, always place one hand under the chest with the forefinger between the front legs, and place the other hand under his bottom.

Flannelized rubber sheeting is an ideal surface for the bottom of the bed for the new puppies. It is inexpensive and washable, and will provide a surface that will give the puppies traction so that they will not slip either while nursing or when learning to walk.

Sometimes the puppies' nails are so long and sharp that they scratch the bitch's breasts. Since the nails are soft, they can be trimmed with ordinary scissors.

At about four weeks of age, formula should be provided. The amount fed each day should be increased over a period of two weeks, when the puppies can be weaned completely. One of the commercially prepared formulas can be mixed according to the directions on the container, or formula can be prepared at home in accordance with instructions from a veterinarian. The formula should be warmed to lukewarm, and poured into a shallow pan placed on the floor of the box. After his mouth has been dipped into the mixture a few times, a puppy will usually start to lap formula. All puppies should be allowed to eat from the same pan, but be sure the small ones get their share. If they are pushed aside, feed them separately. Permit the puppies to nurse part of the time, but gradually increase the number of meals of formula. By the time the puppies are five weeks old, the dam should be allowed with them only at night. When they are about six weeks old, they should be weaned completely. Three meals a day are usually sufficient from this time until the puppies are about three months old, when feedings are reduced to two a day. About the time the dog reaches one year of age, feedings may be reduced to one each day. (For further information on this subject, see page 27.)

Once they are weaned, puppies should be given temporary distemper injections every two weeks until they are old enough for permanent inoculations. At six weeks, stool specimens should be checked for worms, for almost without exception, puppies become infested. Specimens should be checked again at eight weeks, and as often thereafter as your veterinarian recommends.

Sometimes owners decide as a matter of convenience to have a bitch spayed or a male castrated. While this is recommended when a dog has a serious inheritable defect or when abnormalities of reproductive organs develop, in sound, normal purebred dogs, spaying a bitch or castrating a male may prove a definite disadvantage. The operations automatically bar dogs from competing in shows as well as precluding use for breeding. The operations are seldom dangerous, but they should not be performed without serious consideration of these facts.

Using a catheter (tube-feeding) to provide supplemental feeding for the puppy. Note "pet nurser" at left. Supplemental feeding of newborn puppies should not be undertaken unless ABSOLUTELY NECESSARY.

YOUR DOG BOOK SERIES

Illustrated with photographs and line drawings, including chapters on selecting a puppy, famous kennels and dogs, breed history and development, personality and character, training, feeding, grooming, kenneling, breeding, whelping, etc. 5½ x 8½.

YOUR AFGHAN HOUND	YOUR LHASA APSO
YOUR AIREDALE TERRIER	YOUR MALTESE
YOUR ALASKAN MALAMUTE	YOUR MINIATURE PINSCHER
YOUR BASENJI	YOUR NORWEGIAN ELKHOUND
YOUR BEAGLE	YOUR OLD ENGLISH SHEEPDOG
YOUR BORZOI	YOUR PEKINGESE
YOUR BOXER	YOUR POMERANIAN
YOUR BULLDOG	YOUR POODLE
YOUR BULL TERRIER	YOUR PUG
YOUR CAIRN TERRIER	YOUR SAMOYED
YOUR CHIHUAHUA	YOUR SHIH TZU
YOUR DACHSHUND	YOUR SILKY TERRIER
YOUR ENGLISH SPRINGER SPANIEL	YOUR ST. BERNARD
YOUR GERMAN SHEPHERD	YOUR VIZSLA
YOUR GERMAN SHORTHAIRED POINTER	YOUR WELSH CORGI
YOUR GREAT DANE	YOUR YORKSHIRE TERRIER

OTHER DOG BOOKS

THE BEARDED COLLIE	GREAT DANES IN CANADA
THE BELGIAN SHEEPDOG	GROOMING AND SHOWING TOY DOGS
BIRD DOGS AND UPLAND GAME BIRDS	GUIDE TO JUNIOR SHOWMANSHIP
THE BOOK OF DOG GENETICS	HOW TO SPEAK DOG
THE BOSTON TERRIER	HOW TO TRAIN DOGS FOR POLICE WORK
THE BOUVIER DES FLANDRES	THE IRISH TERRIER
BREEDING BETTER COCKER SPANIELS	THE KERRY BLUE TERRIER
THE BRITTANY	THE LABRADOR RETRIEVER
THE BULLMASTIFF	LEADER DOGS FOR THE BLIND
THE CARDIGAN HANDBOOK	THE MASTIFF
THE CHESAPEAKE BAY RETRIEVER	MEISEN BREEDING MANUAL
CHINESE NAMES FOR ORIENTAL DOGS	MEISEN POODLE MANUAL
THE CHINESE SHAR-PEI	MR. LUCKY'S TRICK DOG TRAINING
THE COMPLETE GERMAN SHORTHAIRED POINTER	THE NEWFOUNDLAND
DOG OBEDIENCE TRAINING MANUAL, VOL. 1	THE PHARAOH HOUND
DOG OBEDIENCE TRAINING MANUAL, VOL. 2	THE PORTABLE PET
DOG OBEDIENCE TRAINING MANUAL, VOL. 3	RAPPID OBEDIENCE & WATCHDOG TRAINING
DOGS IN SHAKESPEARE	RUSSIAN NAMES FOR RUSSIAN DOGS
DOGS ON THE FRONTIER	SHOW DOGS—PREPARATION AND PRESENTATION OF
DOG TRAINING IS KID STUFF	SKITCH (The Message of the Roses)
DOG TRAINING IS KID STUFF COLORING BOOK	THE STANDARD BOOK OF DOG BREEDING
THE DYNAMICS OF CANINE GAIT	THE STANDARD BOOK OF DOG GROOMING
GAELIC NAMES FOR CELTIC DOGS	THE STANDARD BOOK OF KENNEL MANAGEMENT
GERMAN NAMES FOR GERMAN DOGS	TOP PRODUCERS—SIBERIAN HUSKYS
THE GOLDEN RETRIEVER	THE UNCOMMON DOG BREEDS
THE GREAT AMERICAN DOG SHOW GAME	YOU AND YOUR IRISH WOLFHOUND

To order any of these books, write to Denlinger's Publishers, P.O. Box 76, Fairfax, VA 22030

For information call (703) 631-1500   VISA and Master Charge orders accepted.

New titles are constantly in production, so please call us to inquire about breed books not listed here.